'Janine is more than an accomplished speaker and author, she truly understands people — at the core, "the why". I am thankful to have her in my tribe, on my path to brilliance. Thank you!'

— **Darren Needham-Walker**, Global Marketing Leader, Developer of high performing teams, across IBM, HP and TechnologyOne

'Janine has this amazing trait of being able to be on the cutting edge of what leaders need to excel and how to support them across the challenges and opportunities leadership brings. Her concept of infectious brilliance is a must read for the contemporary leaders of 2020 and beyond. Entrepreneurs making big bold decisions, corporate leaders who are making broadscale decisions and those who want that extra-factor will gain so much leveraging this book.'

— **Olivia Walsh**, Senior Vice President, Global Head of Talent Management, CBRE

'The world needed this book! *Be Brilliant* is both a guide and a permission slip. Whenever I have the privilege of spending time with Janine, I have renewed confidence and am reminded of my purpose. This book gave me the same feeling. This isn't a technical "how-to" book, but through her storytelling and by sharing her own vulnerabilities Janine is guiding us on our own path to brilliance. She genuinely believes we all have brilliance within us and after reading this book, I'm starting to believe it too! This book is permission to be yourself and share with the world what is uniquely brilliant about us.'

— **Alison Flemming**, General Manager Retail Design & Delivery, Scentre Group

'Janine's book helped me finally understand how important it is to know yourself and how to be your brilliant self. Her book made it so clear and easy to understand. Reading Janine's book gave me clarity on how to show up consistently and how to be my best at all times. The minute I started reading it, I knew it was exactly what I was looking for.'

— **Ronald L. Harvey Sr.**, Vice President, Global Core Strategies and Consulting

'Something became painfully clear as soon as I picked up *Be Brilliant*. How on earth could she step on my toes from half-a-world away? How could she know about my battle against the voices that tell me I should be more than I am? Janine takes us on a masterful, deeply personal, and compelling journey that reminds us that much of what holds us back from our loftiest dreams lies somewhere beneath the noise that we've become accustomed to and in some ways accepted. In *Be Brilliant*, Janine not only challenges everything — every thought… every voice you've listened to for so long — she provides practical tips and tools to step through the noise and move you from where you are to where you really want to be. She teaches us how to truly connect with the world around us as we unleash, within ourselves and others, that which has remained hidden for so long. She reminds us that the world awaits our light — our brilliance!'

— **Michael E. Perry, Ph.D.**, President/Chief Operating Officer,
Human Performance and Behavior Expert

'I have worked with Janine as a partner in our organisation and I have seen her literally "unleash brilliance" in three successive cohorts of our flagship leadership program. When I read this book, I was excited to see what she would be able to do with this topic on paper. I was amazed (although I shouldn't have been) that she was able to convey her passion, commitment and influence in her book in the same way she does in person. Having read the book I found that I was talking to myself a little more, throwing out my comfortable shoes (or at least wearing them less often) and most importantly appreciating that someone told me over and over again that I was brilliant. In a senior role to have that comfort in a book is a wonderful gift and it is one I shall be returning to time and again when I feel my light fading.'

— **Natasha Copley**, Human Resources Director, A&NZ

'Janine Garner is obsessed with helping people achieve their brilliance! Myself and my teams have recently had the privilege of working closely with Janine to "Unleash our Brilliance"! She is fixated with helping people elevate themselves. The way in which she shows us how to build connection and intent through our network, and unleash our unique brilliance, is incredibly inspiring. I have experienced the impact personally and seen the elevation throughout our organisation. I believe her strategies are fundamental to building the leaders of today and tomorrow, which will position people and their companies at the forefront of opportunity.'

— **Derek Macartney**, CEO Preacta Recruitment

'Insightful, instructive and inspiring, this book is a siren call to the brilliance within you! It will embolden you to clear through the mental clutter, connect with your truth, and step fully into the unique brilliance of the person you were born to become. What greater gift is there?'

— **Margie Warrell**, Bestselling author of *You've Got This! The Life-Changing Power of Trusting Yourself*

'Janine Garner's latest book is simply BRILLIANT. Packed with personal stories and relevant insights this is bound to be another bestseller. The reader is guided through an engaging process to help them understand who they are and what they want to become brilliant in. Packed full of tips, techniques and inspiration this book is for anyone who wants to have a better shot of achieving their potential and being a bit more brilliant.'

— **Gabrielle Dolan**, Bestselling author of 5 books on business storytelling and real communication and Founder of Jargon Free Fridays

'Full of real-life stories both her own and many others, this book is just full of LIFE. It's engaging and is a mix of the theory behind being brilliant along with the stories and facts to back it up. I love how Janine both respects and challenges Simon Sinek's "know your why first" and as Janine says in this book — in today's world it is hard to be truly you when there are so many influencing people and things out there telling us we should be someone else rather than ourselves. Our true selves. I have read Janine's previous books and I truly believe this is the best work she has produced. I enjoyed every word — her commentary, her learnings, and her humour completely shined through and I loved how she walked her own talk by sharing her stories too, not just others! Standing in her spotlight and empowering others to do the same! This is brilliant and I know it will empower others to see their own brilliance too!'

— **Michelle Sutherland**, Social Entrepreneur and National Vice President, Arbonne

'In a world of relentless competition and crazy diaries, Janine's wisdom is the sanity check that smart people are desperate for. Her raw honesty and care for others' success make her a powerhouse both on stage and in writing. This book is smart, funny and as brilliant as the name suggests.'

— **Ray Pittman**, President & Chief Operating Officer,
McWHINNEY

'I started reading *Be Brilliant* and simply couldn't put it down! This book is beautifully written, and it's packed full of techniques and strategies to help you embrace your authenticity. Janine's four laws of brilliance are indeed clarifying and will absolutely inspire you to own the power you have to create and lead a more fulfilled life. The lessons in this book fuel introspection at a deep level. After reading it, you will understand that you are made more brilliant, not less, by embracing the whole of who you are — the flaws, the strengths, the failures and the successes. Leaders who want to unleash the brilliance within themselves and their teams need to grab this book today and discover how to advance to the next level, personally and professionally.'

— **Terina Allen**, CEO, ARVis Institute and Chair, Strategic Leadership
Network, Columnist, Forbes Media

'If you want to be a better leader of yourself and others via maximising the brilliance within you, then this book will help you find a way forward. A must-read for anyone wanting to fulfil their biggest ambitions.'

— **Kate Mason**, Group Director, People & Culture,
Coca Cola Amatil

Be Brilliant

Be Brilliant

HOW TO LEAD
A LIFE OF INFLUENCE

Janine Garner

BESTSELLING AUTHOR of *IT'S WHO YOU KNOW*

WILEY

First published in 2020 by John Wiley & Sons Australia, Ltd
42 McDougall St, Milton Qld 4064
Office also in Melbourne

Typeset in Utopia Std Regular 10.5/14pt

© John Wiley & Sons Australia, Ltd 2020

The moral rights of the author have been asserted

ISBN: 978-0-730-38376-5

A catalogue record for this book is available from the National Library of Australia

Cover design: Wiley

Cover image: © Shutterstock/Glitterstudio

Internal illustrations: Ellie Schroeder — Creation Alchemist

Author photo: Oli Sansom

Printed in the United States of America by Quad/Graphics

VDED4C7FB-9015-4007-A1C5-C2DE023D9341_070120

Disclaimer
The material in this publication is of the nature of general comment only, and does not represent professional advice. It is not intended to provide specific guidance for particular circumstances and it should not be relied on as the basis for any decision to take action or not take action on any matter which it covers. Readers should obtain professional advice where appropriate, before making any such decision. To the maximum extent permitted by law, the author and publisher disclaim all responsibility and liability to any person, arising directly or indirectly from any person taking or not taking action based on the information in this publication.

Contents

About Janine

Janine is obsessed with unleashing the brilliance in individuals, teams and companies. As a connection expert at the organisational level (collaboration), interpersonal level (networking) and intrapersonal level (energy and intent), her whole world revolves around helping others reclaim and reignite their influence.

A highly sought-after keynote speaker, educator and author, Janine works with high-profile global leaders, and helps many of Australia's top 50 ASX companies and multinationals — EY, CBRE, DXC Technology, Hewlett-Packard, Micro Focus, Optus and CBA, to name a few.

Janine is the best-selling author of *It's Who You Know: How a network of 12 key people can fast-track your success* and *From Me to We: Why commercial collaboration will future-proof business, leaders and personal success.*

She also holds a Bachelor of Science degree from Aston University, UK, and was awarded an Honorary Doctorate of Science from the same university in 2016. She is a graduate of the Harvard Kennedy School in 'The Art and Practice of Leadership', a partner at Thought Leaders Global and has won an International Stevie Award in recognition of her work.

On top of this, Janine is super proud to have completed two Tough Mudders and one Spartan race and relishes the hardest challenge of all: raising three teenage children.

In addition to television and radio gigs, Janine also has her thoughts and insights published regularly in the media at *HuffPost*, *CEO Magazine*, *Success* magazine, *BRW*, Women's Agenda, AIM and *The Australian*. She is also the host of her own podcast, *Unleashing Brilliance*, featuring the untold stories of individual successes from people around the world.

Janine believes we need people, teams and companies to be absolutely brilliant to lead today's complex environment into tomorrow's unknowns. This requires collaboration, transformation and leverage and it demands better conversations, training and connection.

That's the power you have when you are your brilliant self.

Janinegarner.com.au

Acknowledgements

To the most precious people in my world—Jason, Flynn, Taya and Carter—thank you for always loving me for being me and inspiring me every day to become a better person. I love you all so much.

To my amazing inner circle of friends and colleagues who continue to challenge my thinking, encourage me to keep going and who are always there for a glass of bubbles to celebrate and a hug when needed—I am forever grateful knowing you are in my corner and cheering me on from the sidelines.

To the many brilliant leaders, clients and thinkers that have allowed me to share their stories and learnings in these pages and on my podcast—our conversations planted the initial seeds of thinking behind this book. Thank you for being brave enough to share your personal stories, wisdom and insight so that others can learn too.

To Kelly Irving—you really are a genius wordsmith. Your patience and encouragement always pushed me to go deeper and further in my thinking and your ideas have helped shape this book into what it has become. I am forever grateful for all you do and for all you are.

To the wider team that have worked on bringing my words to life — Lucy Raymond, Ingrid Bond, Sandra Balonyi, Bronwyn Evans and the entire team at Wiley, Ellie Schroeder for your awesome designs and Scott Eathorne for your media magic. A massive thank you for continuing to believe in me.

To each of you — thank you for taking the time to read this book; to being open to becoming more brilliant. My wish for you is that this book opens up a whole new world of opportunity for you to become even more brilliant in all you do.

Introduction

How do you feel about the future? Be honest... because most of us would agree that the mere thought is simply exhausting.

- It's *exhausting* trying to keep pace with technological changes.

- It's *exhausting* keeping on top of other people's lives: our teams, our families, our children, our friends.

- It's *exhausting* trying to keep up with work demands and the changing business landscape.

- It's *exhausting* having to conform to industry, societal and — let's be honest — social-media expectations of how to look, be and behave.

- It's *exhausting* trying to prove that we're good enough.

- It's *exhausting* trying to perform and play a bigger game.

- It's *exhausting* being human in today's busy world.

When everything external to us is moving so quickly, the risk is we enter a space of feeling out of control; we worry about what we don't have and seek out solutions to band-aid our perceived imperfections and doubts. We regress into a space of *me*, of self-protection, of 'protect what I know, learn what I don't and until then I'll fake it till I make it'.

We look externally for options to invest in learning and programs to improve our skills and capabilities. We buy tools and expertise to improve performance. We spend hours researching the next big thing so we can be ahead of the curve. And we invest materially in external validations of success.

We want to be in demand, to be needed, to be relevant, to be seen as successful, so we spend a fortune on stuff, on shit, that we think will make us 'better' — that will 'fix us'.

And what does this really get us?

Despite this constant acquisition of skills, work, promotions, learning, material possessions and jam-packed calendars, there are so many of us living daily with imposter-like feelings, doubts of our own abilities and questions about the path we're on.

Despite a perception of increased connectedness thanks to the quantitative counting of friends and connections online, and time spent scrolling, we're living increasingly in an age of loneliness and depression — of disconnection from ourselves and who we want to be.

And despite the outward appearance of being in control, stress, mental health and disengagement levels are at an all-time high in the workplace and at home. Relationships are breaking down, both with our team members at work and our family and mates at home.

We feel uninspired by leaders, organisations, brands, governments and businesses. We question the type of leader, partner, parent, friend and person we want to be.

Worse yet, in this fast-moving new world, we're having to learn to live with incessant change. Talent is no longer enough, truths are hard to find and being fake is more visible; yet somehow, we're expected to live and lead a brilliant life.

How on earth can we be brilliant — and feel brilliant — when we're engulfed by disillusionment, comparison-itis, blame-itis, imposter syndrome-itis and lack of self-belief-itis?

Why this book — why now?

These are just some of the examples of *internal* pressures we put ourselves under. What about the *external* ones?

Here's what we're facing.

Problem 1: business was simple; now it's competitive

Business used to be relatively easy. We'd work on our one-, three- and five-year plans. We'd present them for sign-off and then off we'd go, like good little soldiers, implementing them. Life felt uncomplicated. Business felt uncomplicated — calm, simple, known — and the speed of change felt considered.

But now we're living in extraordinary times of change and challenge. Business is more complex than ever before, and we're no longer performing on a level playing field. We're not just competing locally in our own backyard, we're competing nationally and globally for everything: resources, people, sales and profit.

Problem 2: clients were easy; now they're demanding

Likewise, our clients and suppliers used to be relatively easy-going. In fact, we loved hanging out with them. Want to head out for a spot of lunch? Sure, why not? Can we meet to discuss our business terms and plans for the next year? Of course, let's have a chat.

But now our clients, suppliers, employees and leaders are becoming more demanding, wanting everything better, quicker and cheaper. And if you can't deliver on this you'd better throw in some extra services and value—for free, of course!

And it's not just *them*—it's *us*! We get annoyed if our Uber doesn't turn up in 90 seconds, if we can't get the cheapest flight on offer, that table booked in the new super-cool restaurant, one-hour delivery of that must-have dress for the weekend—and get a replacement within 24 hours.

Problem 3: communication was straight-forward; now it's overwhelming

Marketing used to be a four-step process. Once we'd diagnosed the '4Ps' of our marketing plan—product, price, promotion and place—we'd allocate our marketing dollars across a limited range of options: television, radio, print and maybe a promotional event or two.

Now we're operating in an increasingly interconnected, fast and flat world that allows us to market anything, everywhere. As long as you have a phone and a laptop you can get your brand out there from anywhere, at any time and in any place. We're bombarded daily with information that we're attempting to process and compete with. Technology has changed how we connect, interact, work and relate—it's changing how we exist.

Problem 4: resources were limitless; now they're stretched

In the 1990s, when I started work, resources were limitless. It was the time of the banking boom in London: the champagne flowed, company credit cards were put behind the bar with free abandon. We could even access the stationery cupboard without asking for a key and print A3 in colour (shock horror!) without worrying about being caught by the office manager.

Now everything has been cut—resources, headcounts, budgets, travel—and we're watched as if under a microscope. Despite the cuts, we're all under the pump to do more with less.

Problem 5: employment was secure; now it's uncertain

Remember when a job was for life? You were embedded into the company, secure in the knowledge that you would be looked after until the day you retired.

But with changing industries, evolving organisational structures, technological advancements changing the jobs available, increased competition across generations and the necessity to upskill, reskill and evolve skills based on the future of work, jobs are no longer guaranteed. In fact, recent research states that millennials will have 17 different jobs in their lifetime! Eek!

Without each other, without collaboration and connection, without us all being our absolute best, we can't adapt and move at the speed needed to meet these demands.

Better be yourself

We all have to get better at being ourselves.

Think about it: without people being who they truly are, being their brilliant selves, we'll never create the true heart and soul, the belonging that's needed to turn the challenges of our present into the successes of our future. When we reconnect and reclaim who we are in the entirety of our lived experience, imperfections and strengths, and when we stop faking it till we make it, we'll be in a position to unleash our individual brilliance, and at the same time unleash the brilliance in others.

So, the solution here is to start by looking at *who*.

In 2009, Simon Sinek published his first book, *Start with Why,* which included the infamous Golden Circle framework for his approach to leadership — that 'people don't buy *what* you do; they buy *why* you do it'.

While Sinek was undoubtedly correct in identifying a starting point for why you're doing something, this thinking has created a tsunami of significant unrest and anxiety as people and organisations try to find their purpose in life.

What do we value? What's our mission? Why are we here? These are the questions we ask ourselves on a daily basis — and if we don't have the answers, we panic!

While I'm absolutely not discrediting his great work, what I am proposing is that there are other, more critical questions that need to be asked first: Who are you? Who are you being and who do you want to become?

Understanding *why* on its own will never work.

The *who* we are and who we want to become and the *why* we're doing what we're doing must align, otherwise there will always be a point of tension and conflict.

Phil Knight, founder of Nike, talks to this concept in his book *Shoe Dog*. He writes about what sparked his success at selling. After being unable to sell encyclopedias because he hated it, and feeling empty inside when selling mutual funds, he started selling shoes and realised he enjoyed it because 'it wasn't selling': he believed in running and believed these were the best shoes to run in and that the 'world would be a better place' if people ran every day. He added, 'People, sensing my belief, wanted some of that belief for themselves. Belief, I decided. Belief is irresistible'.

What Knight shared is that the *why* for other people only became important when he had *belief* in himself — in his *who* — first.

So, what if we could remove the shackles we're placing on ourselves and instead know that we have all we need *right now*? That we have all the skill and capability that's needed to contribute and influence; that our opinion matters; that the culmination of all the facets of ourselves — the strengths, the weaknesses, the successes, the failures, the loves and the imperfections — are our perfectly imperfect and brilliant selves.

We just need to tap into it! Embrace it!

You have all that you need to be brilliant.

To meet all of your challenges and demands head-on, right now.

It starts with *you*.

My wish for you, as a reader of this book, is to understand that we're all unique, that we all have individual facets that, when embraced, will help us become the best individuals, partners, parents, leaders, team and organisations we can be.

Much like learning how to meditate for hours or mastering a one-handed push-up, it takes continuous work to be brilliant, work that lasts a lifetime! But this continuous mastery, ongoing improvement and determination to become better is where the opportunity exists for you and for those you lead.

Only when we take ownership of who we are, who we want to be and who we want to become, only when we accept all of our imperfections and rise above our limitations, only when we unleash our own inner brilliance can we truly create the space for others to do the same.

Brilliance is infectious.

So, let's be brilliant together.

The quest to be brilliant

I was born to a working-class, farming family in a small village called Guiseley in Yorkshire in the north of England. My dad was a poultry farmer and my stay-at-home mum juggled kids, the farm and the market on weekends. While riding around on my dad's lap on the tractor, he would often say (in his strong northern accent) 'Where there's muck there's brass, love', which meant, 'if you put in the hard work, the money will come'.

Mum, on the other hand, would share her pride at being 'the first girl in the family' to attend Leeds secretarial college and then the disappointment at having to give it all up when she got married.

Something many people don't know about me is that I received a full student grant and financial support from the government to go to university. There's no way my farming family could have funded my further education without this. Suddenly, I was off (hooray!). I packed my backpack and headed to Birmingham, not realising at the time that I would never return home to live again.

I remember that first term—the conversations, the people, their backgrounds—my eyes were well and truly opened to the world of possibility, and also to self-doubt, lack of confidence, imposter syndrome, imperfection and all of my flaws.

I worked and played hard and graduated four years later with a Bachelor of Science, a significant amount of debt, some lifelong friends and a suitcase full of memories. Over the next eight years, in London this time, I tackled the ongoing, exhausting battle between striving for more and proving I was good enough. I was determined to 'make it in a man's world' and prove to my dad that I could do it.

Despite rising through the ranks, self-doubt always told me I wasn't smart enough, savvy enough, brave enough or good enough to be there.

By the age of 27, I'd fallen in love with an Aussie, Jason, and decided to run away from those nagging doubts and try again — somewhere new. I left my job, sold my belongings, packed my backpack (again) and moved to Australia.

Over the next 10 years, I rebuilt my career in a country where I had no friends and no proof of who I was or what I could achieve. I lived on the verge of burnout and breakdown while juggling three young children, a full-time corporate job and horrendous bullying at a senior level. Deciding I'd had enough I chose to leave to set up and bootstrap my own business.

Then, my husband's company went into receivership and he lost his job. With no regular money coming in we hit rock bottom financially. We had to sell up, downsize to a rental, live off credit cards — we even went as far as having conversations with mates about camping in their backyards (I'm serious!).

Through it all, Jason believed in me — that was all the fuel I needed to open my eyes and make a change. I took back control and I worked. I dug deep, I hustled and I invested in the right people around me to keep me focused and on track. I formed the LBDGroup, a network for commercially smart women who collaborate and support each other (which I sold in March 2019).

Since then, I've built a global speaking and training business, working with some of the most inspiring businesses and leaders who are committed to driving change in industry. In 2011 I founded the not-for-profit First Seeds Fund with an incredible board of women who, together, helped many parents and kids in disadvantaged areas in Australia. I became a partner at Thought Leaders Global, a business helping clever people become commercially smart. In 2017, I received an Honorary Doctorate of Science from the University of Aston in Birmingham and was privileged to be asked to speak to the graduating year of students. I've even written and published two books (one of which is a bestseller — let's hope this third one becomes one, too).

Why am I telling you this? It's not about stroking my own ego, telling you all the things I'm good at, or all that I've done. No, it's about owning the good stuff — the achievements *and* the nagging internal voices along the way — everything I've told myself I'm not doing 'right' or could do 'better' (like writing this book).

Just like you, my journey was never and will never be all unicorns and rainbows. That's not life.

Being brilliant is about accepting the conditioning we've grown up with, why we think the way we do, recognising what drives us, celebrating our wins, *and* equally, recognising when we're being hard on ourselves, when we judge ourselves and when we fu*k up!

I know, I know, easier said than done, right?

Like me, you've probably spent *years* investing in yourself, reading self-development books, going on training programs to make you a better leader, negotiator, writer, presenter, thinker (insert whatever works for you). And even after all this investment, you continue to question who you are and what you're doing. *It's crazy!* We continue to question our worth and our brilliance! Why?

Barriers to our brilliance

We're struggling with owning who we are and giving ourselves permission to become our best selves. We're wanting to belong but feeling lonely.

And while we talk about collaboration and building teams, we're so worried about ourselves that we're continuing to operate from a place of *me* versus a place of togetherness, of us, of *we*.

We're all at risk of becoming the robots of life versus the humans of extraordinary evolution, where potential is unleashed and brilliance shines.

The world is asking us to be our extraordinary, brilliant selves, but we're not listening. Instead, we're suffering with extreme and multidimensional fatigue at three levels:

1. *exhaustion fatigue* — we're exhausted with being exhausted

2. *stretch fatigue* — we're pulled in 101 directions, often at the same time, by multiple parties

3. *choice fatigue* — we struggle with what to do next, tomorrow, the day after; first, second, at the same time, or all *right now!*

Ring true?

Exhaustion fatigue

We feel exhausted every day with all that we have to do and by the thought of the future and what we think we 'should' be doing. You may even now be starting to spin as you think about what you should be doing right now instead of reading this book.

There's too much to do and not enough time. We're racing around putting out fires, answering emails, attending meetings, meeting demands, rushing around like headless chickens trying to look the part and act the part, but maybe not quite delivering in a way that's sustainable for us over the longer term — and we know it.

Downtime is becoming increasingly limited. On-time is becoming increasingly maximised. We spin out of control, running ourselves ragged, falling under the pressure of the demands of adaptability, agility and connectivity.

We face chronic exhaustion from the pressures to keep up and this mental, emotional and physical tiredness is interfering with our levels of happiness and personal fulfilment, our relationships and our ability to work effectively and navigate the options and choices in front of us.

It's simply exhausting being human!

Stretch fatigue

So many of us are operating like a real-life version of 'Elastigirl'. We're pulled and pushed, stretched and re-stretched in multiple directions by multiple groups of multiple people all demanding work and a whole stack of other stuff that needs to be done ASAP. Everyone and everything wants you, and wants you *now*.

Add to this whatever role or roles you currently have that you're feeling guilty about. For example, 'Janine, as a mother you really *should* be cooking a healthy dinner every night for your kids; Janine, you really *should* be spending more time with friends; Janine you really *shouldn't* be outsourcing all those home chores because you *should* be doing them'.

Whether we're single, partnered, a parent or not, we're enrolled in the University of Juggle Town, attempting to successfully achieve a PhD in Time Management, Multitasking and Getting Shit Done (ugh).

Choice fatigue

This job or that job? To hire or to fire? To say 'yes' or 'no'? To stay quiet or to speak up? This media platform or that platform? Which course? Which holiday? Which diet? This decision or that decision? To stay the same? To change direction? To sell or to buy? To stay or to go?

The more choices we're faced with, the more exhausted we become as we weigh up all the options in an attempt to make the right decision (if there is ever such a thing as 'right').

Then, when we make the choice, we doubt our decision, and we swing between self-doubt and self-denial. We enter the world of comparison — seeking out and seeing those who are doing better than us, who we perceive have made the better choice. Our imposter syndrome kicks in when we don't believe we're good enough to have made the choice we've made, and we worry about being found out. And suddenly that spiral of indecision starts again.

Ultimately all we really want is to be *in flow*: for life to be easy, tension-free, for the friction of too much choice to be removed so we can just get on with it.

Stick your hand up please

How many of these do you admit to feeling on a daily basis? (Go on, tick them off.)

- fear about what you're doing or if you can even do 'it'

- self-doubt as to whether you're 'good enough'

- imposter syndrome: 'I shouldn't be here'

- comparing yourself to others who may be 'doing it better'

- blaming yourself for not 'being there yet'

- questioning what you're doing and why (again)

- telling yourself negative stories about what will happen if you do or don't

- feeling worn out and wanting to give up

- running away from it all!

We don't think we're cut out for this!

Tick, tick.

Undertaking any meaningful endeavour — launching a business, building a new product offering, expanding your team, entering a new market, writing a book, developing a new website — requires you to be at your best. It requires you to be brilliant — and yes, this is often easier said than done.

All of us start with the best intentions, but our diaries and commitments to ourselves get taken over by someone or something else. The distractions are on continuous play, challenging our focus. The messages about conforming are on steroids — be the thinnest, smartest, healthiest, most productive, youngest, richest — challenging our desire to just be me.

I acknowledge that even now as a mother of three, wife, sister, daughter, friend, these inner demons continue to raise their ugly heads. I'm not brilliant. I have flaws and imperfections — too many to list here.

But what I have learned is to accept who I am and be pretty gentle and forgiving of myself. I've learned that I have certain strengths where I can add a lot of value, and equally, I have a hell of a lot of weaknesses that are hard to change. I've learned to accept all of this about myself, and I've learned to get curious about my behaviours, and about how and why some people get under my skin. I've learned to continually lead from a place of courage and acceptance of others, of loving unconditionally and teaching always.

It's not easy though — after all, I've got many years of my own unconscious bias, ideas and opinions, as do you. But when we give in to the inner demons and negative voices, we can't do our best work. We can't bring the best of ourselves to what we do, and we can't do what it is we want to do and achieve with our life.

Truth be told, we can't lead others or bring out the best in others until we lead ourselves.

The 4 laws of brilliance

Like a diamond with hundreds of different facets and flaws, I believe our unique individualisms can be 'cut and polished'. And only when we can lead ourselves, accepting our imperfections and rising above our limitations (of which we all have many) can we live a life of influence and magnify the same in others.

And much like the brilliance of a diamond takes artistry and workmanship to bring out the brightness and the contrast, we have to do the craftmanship on ourselves to bring our best selves to all that we do.

It is the angle at which light enters the diamond and is reflected back that creates the brilliance: too shallow and the light isn't bright enough; too deep and the light becomes dull. The same can be said of us. If we fake it till we make it, only showing the part of ourselves that we think is acceptable, our bullshit will be seen by others. Alternatively, the more real and authentic we can become, the braver we can be to show who we really are, and the more we can shine brightly in how we live and lead; how we influence, connect and collaborate.

We need to own the sharp angles and blemishes. We need to understand that we all come in different shapes, sizes and colours. For some of us the blemishes and imperfections are close to the surface, for some they are hidden deep down, and for others they are disguised, hidden from the world. But every facet of who we are is our uniqueness and brilliance. As one of my clients, Suzanne Rohr, shared during a workshop, 'We are all rare gems designed to shine, created under enormous pressure'.

There are four laws to live and lead by if we want to be our brilliant selves.

1. *Be You*: Own your spotlight

2. *Be Ready*: Harness your energy

3. *Be Together*: Connect with intent

4. *Be Heard*: Magnify your influence

Each law is made up of three facets (see figure 1).

Each of the four sections of this book deals with one law. As you begin reading each section, I'll ask you to identify how you're doing right now in relation to that law. Be honest with yourself. Ask yourself what's working and what's not working.

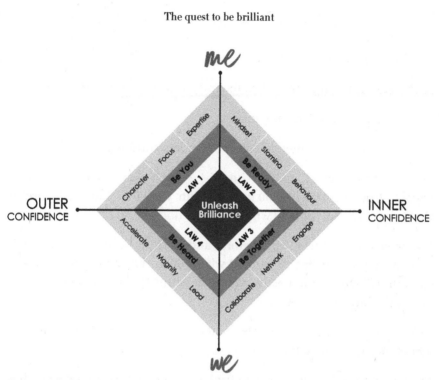

Figure 1: the Unleash Brilliance model

You're unlikely to find that you'll nail all four laws at the same time. You'll always be kicking goals in some areas and needing to do work in others. You'll find that you're strong on some laws and weak on others. Naturally, the key is to maintain the strengths and strengthen the weak areas.

Make sure you keep coming back to the Unleash Brilliance model and each of the laws to understand where you need to harness your focus.

For this to work there are some key requirements:

◆ Be curious.

◆ Take ownership of what's going on.

◆ Do the work to move forward.

For this to go wrong:

- ◆ stay stuck in your ways believing you already know this stuff

- ◆ remain closed to change

- ◆ resist being challenged on your current thinking.

Given you've picked up this book, I reckon the latter three don't exist — although at points you may go 'yeah, yeah I've read this before'. If that's the case, ask yourself why you're not doing it.

You may say, 'I've tried this before, and it didn't work'. Well, if that's true, were you curious to explore what got in the way? Did you learn something? Did you honestly take ownership? Or did you give up? Try again. Explore another way.

I use this model in training and coaching to help individuals identify where they need to do the work.

I use it on myself when I feel in a funk or stuck, as I try to uncover what the real problem is.

I use this model at the start of every year to reset and refocus, to get back in control of myself and back on track with what I'm trying to achieve personally and professionally.

Remember, brilliance is a practice, so use this model and the 'Brilliance in action' exercises at the end of each law for yourself, your team and your family.

Do the work and the work will take care of itself.

Let's begin.

Law 1: Be You

Own your spotlight

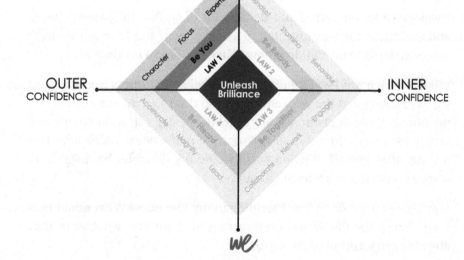

Own all the facets that make you, you.
Become positioned and known for all you are and all you do.
Your consistency, passion and conviction in yourself become infectious.
And as others see the real you, the multiplier effect of your impact kicks in.

When my children Flynn, Taya and Carter were seven, five and three respectively, both my husband and I were working full-time. The morning pre-work juggle was insane as we rushed around trying to drop the children at before-school care and day care, leaving just enough time to get to work. If any of the kids were sick then all hell would break loose as we negotiated with each other who had the most to lose that day, who could stay home and care for said child... and God help us if the sickness passed from one to the other...

I remember one particular evening sitting down to have dinner as a family and during the 'How was your day?' conversation Taya asked me, 'Mummy, why are you always so busy?'

'Well,' I said. 'I've worked hard to get through school and university, I have a degree, I've built my career so that we have money to buy what we want — your toys and clothes — so that we can enjoy holidays'.

She continued, 'But Mummy, why are you so unhappy?'

Boom! It was a stake to my heart. That moment I realised my five year old was right.

I was existing, operating and doing a lot of stuff — but I wasn't living and leading in the way I wanted to live and lead, and I certainly wasn't demonstrating to my children how to live and lead a brilliant life.

What message was I was sending to my daughter? Mummy works so hard she is exhausted at the weekend, she's too tired to play, she's always on her phone, she gets grumpy really quickly, she can't sit still with me and watch *Toy Story* without multitasking. She really doesn't look like she's looking after herself. Why on earth would my daughter be inspired to want a career if that's what it's about?

Equally, what message was I sending to my two boys? What about how I was living my life would be inspiring to them and what were they absorbing in terms of life lessons?

This was a watershed moment for me to take back control and self-ownership. I needed to reconnect and reclaim who I was and who I wanted to be so that I could ultimately influence and lead in a different way.

In a Thrive Global blog, 'The joy of sleep', Arianna Huffington discusses the concept of discovering our true value and the need to know ourselves first and foremost. She says, 'to know yourself, you have to make time to disconnect from the world, so you connect with yourself. That will make it much easier to know what you truly value and then make decisions about what to undertake'.

Owning our individual spotlight is key to success today and tomorrow.

I appreciate this is easier said than done. That the sheer concept of being 100 per cent who you are is tricky. I mean, let's be honest. We all start out with the best intentions, don't we? Remember the dreams you had for yourself as you were growing up, or when you finally graduated and stepped out in the world? Remember when you decided what type of leader or business owner you would be? Remember the things you used to do that would make you laugh so much your face would start hurting? Remember that feeling of dancing like nobody is watching?

Being ourselves is beaten out of us: in the playground by the schoolyard bully, in the workplace by the queen bees and the wannabees, on the back of 360 performance reviews that focus on our weaknesses or what we haven't done. Or maybe you can still remember how you felt after receiving the negative feedback someone once gave you.

Here's the thing though: your business, your team and your family need you to be the best version of yourself so they can be the best versions of themselves too.

Speaker and author, Steve Maraboli says in his book *Unapologetically You*,

> *We all make mistakes, have struggles, and even regret things in our past. But you are not your mistakes, you are not your struggles, and you are here NOW with the power to shape your day and your future.*

This is the focus of Law 1, Be You: Own your spotlight. It's only by practising this that we can become confident about what we're bringing, have the conviction and passion about what we're doing and ultimately be remembered for the impact we're individually making.

Your leadership starts with you reconnecting and reclaiming who you are in your entirety and owning who you ultimately want to be. Hoping to get better is not a strategy!

You have to own the facets that make you, you. You have to start from the inside out.

So where are you at now in your professional life?

Let's start with a little self-reflection to see how you currently rate yourself in terms of whether you're owning your spotlight.

Take a look at this diagram. Where do you feel you are right now in your professional life?

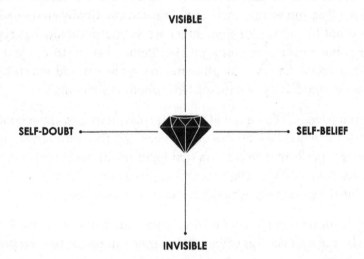

- *Invisible or visible?* Thinking about the work you're doing right now, where would you place yourself along the axis of invisible to visible?

  - Do you feel invisible right now, not being noticed for what you're doing or the value you're adding? Maybe you're even questioning whether you're doing the right thing, in the right job, or you may be questioning if you're even on the right path.

✦ Or are you feeling excited, lit up and getting noticed the majority of the time for what it is that you do? Are you visible?

◆ *Self-doubt or self-belief?* Now, where would you place yourself on the axis of self-doubt to self-belief?

✦ Are you struggling with self-doubt or feelings of 'not good enough'? Maybe you're starting to feel like an imposter in your role and worrying that you don't have what it takes to do the job.

✦ Or are you feeling confident in yourself, your skills and capabilities? You know what you're good at and you're actually feeling good about yourself.

Now grab a pen and draw an 'X' on the spot that you feel best represents where you're at.

Done it?

(Seriously, do it now before we move ahead!)

What do you notice?

You may be feeling really visible right now with your work, the company, even the people you're working with, but the self-doubt and feelings of not being good enough are starting to creep in. You may be questioning your decisions or doubting your capability and so find yourself placing an 'X' in the top left-hand quadrant.

Alternatively, you may be feeling invisible and frustrated at your lack of progress and not getting noticed at work or in the marketplace. You know there's more — you're just maybe not sure what the 'more' is. Your self-belief and conviction are strong but there's just something — you don't know what — that's missing. If this is the case, you may find you place an 'X' in the bottom right-hand quadrant.

Our ultimate aim is to place ourselves in the top right-hand quadrant. A place where we're being noticed for the work we're doing, fired up to do more, where our self-belief is strong, and we know we're doing work we love in the best way we can.

This is a place of owning it: a place of self-ownership.

You'll be unable to consistently inspire others or create the impact you desire until you can take ownership of who you are and the work you're doing.

Once you can identify where you're at, you can identify what you need to focus on to improve and move forward.

The 3 facets of Law 1

In one of my favourite movies, *The Matrix*, the main character (Neo) meets The Oracle and walks under a sign that reads *Temet Nosce*, Latin for 'Know Thyself'. This is the essence of Law 1: that only by getting clear on who you are and owning it — constantly exploring, reflecting and knowing that your inner belief and knowledge is what others will see — will you keep growing.

This is reinforced in multiple articles and studies including the 2009 study, 'The longitudinal impact of self-efficacy and career goals on objective and subjective career success' (*Journal of Vocational Behavior*). The key finding was that self-efficacy (or the belief in oneself) is positively correlated to later career satisfaction and career success.

Let's now look in detail at the three facets that Law 1 addresses:

- ◆ Character
- ◆ Focus
- ◆ Expertise.

Facet 1

Character

One of my all-time favourite childhood movies is *The Wizard of Oz*. It's the story of four friends journeying together, but on individual missions to enhance their own brilliance. Like the wonderful cowardly lion: 'Put 'em up, put 'em up!' he says, bouncing on the spot with his fists balled up. 'Courage! If I only had courage!'

Let's be honest, there are times when all of us could do with a trip down that yellow brick road to find the courage to be ourselves. But like the great and powerful Wizard of Oz says when they finally make it to the Emerald City, 'You, my friend, are a victim of disorganised thinking. You are under the unfortunate impression that just because you run away you have no courage; you're confusing courage with wisdom'.

Just like the lion, we need to reorganise our thinking and self-belief, to recognise that we already have everything we need to be our brilliant selves.

The last couple of years of my corporate life were far from the champagne-popping joyous existence it once was. On paper I had it all — responsibility for good brands, a great salary with awesome job perks — but behind this was an environment of bullying, lying, deceit and game-playing, which meant I was always on the look-out for the next grenade being thrown my way.

I unconsciously absorbed the energy and behaviour of others and ended up leading from my own place of fear and self-protection in an effort to keep one step ahead. It was exhausting and in conflict with my personal values. I was unhappy and a person even I didn't like.

For things to change, I had to go back to the basics of understanding who I was, what I wanted to do and how I wanted to be. I spent months working with a number of coaches, uncovering layer upon layer of who I was and why, and at the same time actually adding to my understanding of who I wanted to be.

The only way I could do my best work and be my best self was to give myself permission to be a non-Instagrammable version of me.

I had to stop wearing the multiple hats of my life and adopting whatever I thought I was 'supposed to be' because, quite frankly, it was getting exhausting. I had to work hard to quit reading into things, creating stories and scenarios of what may be going on, and instead step forward with courage into a place of personal vulnerability and trust.

And so, when I finally left my corporate job, I decided I was going to live, lead and operate on the assumption that people generally were good and ultimately wanted to do the right thing. Now I get that some of you may think this is an unrealistic ideal for the competitive business world. But I truly believe that operating from a place where you assume the majority of people are good, versus evil and out to get you, trip you up, or make you look stupid for their benefit, will bring more joy.

And it has.

From the moment I let go of the pretence and instead took ownership of who I was, the actions I took, the results I achieved and the mistakes I made, I started connecting more deeply with others. I have built relationships that matter; doors have opened for me and for others who were previously invisible. I've engaged in thought-provoking and intelligent debates, worked through challenges with clients from a place of understanding, and my business and personal success and achievement have grown exponentially.

For example, I was recently invited to speak on the topic of 'Unleashing Brilliance' to an audience of about 3000 people in Sydney. I'd prepped my keynote, submitted the slides a few days before and was ready to go.

But on the morning of the keynote I woke up and just knew it was time to be a little bit braver. It was time to replace some of the business case studies of other people I usually shared with stories of myself. I had to dig deep, become a little bit more vulnerable and open up more to show people in the audience that the things I was sharing were on the back of the highs and lows I've learned from my own life and leadership journey. The response was incredible.

> ## Here's the thing: the more we can share of ourselves, and our flaws, the more we touch the hearts and minds of others.

Paul Zahra, non-executive director, board and company advisor and one of Australia's most influential diversity advocates, shared with me during a podcast interview, 'The key message from me today is not changing who you are but rather celebrating your differences and understanding you are unique. Fitting in can be negative and destructive. People have to be very careful about not working hard to fit in, but actually working hard to bring their difference to the workplace'.

So, ask yourself honestly:

- Who are you really being?
- Are you truly being you in everything you do, or have you become someone you don't recognise anymore? Someone, even, you may not like?
- What needs to change to turn that around?

You're the key

Ray Pittman is a C-suite leader in the property industry and has worn many hats throughout his corporate career. I had the pleasure of working with Ray when he was the President and CEO of CBRE Australia and New Zealand. One day I asked him, out of curiosity, what he has learned about himself over his career. He told me, 'I guess to accept who I am and to be pretty gentle and forgiving with myself'.

Ray shared that he was hard and critical on himself during his twenties and thirties, always thinking he wasn't good enough or should be doing more. He added, 'I think as I've gotten older and more experienced, I've realised who I am. I have certain strengths which can really add value. I have certain weaknesses that I'm not going to change. I've learned to accept that about myself and to really focus on what I am good at. Underlying it all is to just be accepting of yourself and not get down if you make a mistake or criticise yourself'.

Your character is what makes you, *you*.

It's what distinguishes you from everyone else. It's your personal currency, your strength, your uniqueness and your opportunity all wrapped up in one amazing package.

Like Ray, you need to accept yourself and focus on the things you're absolutely brilliant at; these are very likely to be the things that you love. And if you're building on the things that you love then you're going to step into a greater, higher place. One where you're able to align who you are, what you think and feel, with the actions you take. This helps you operate from a place of truth and authenticity, which is what others are drawn to.

Alternatively, if you're unclear about who you are, if you're faking it till you make it and changing your behaviours to fit in to any given scenario, then people around you won't believe you, let alone follow you — and you'll start feeling pretty crappy in the end too.

If we don't start leading from within, giving ourselves permission to be who we are, owning our unique values and beliefs, our strengths and our weaknesses and acknowledging the person we are on the inside, imperfections and all, we'll never be capable of being the better person on the outside.

Steve Jobs echoed this thinking when he said, 'Have the courage to follow your heart and intuition. They somehow already know what you truly want to become. Everything else is secondary.'

While John Wooden, UCLA basketball coach, advised, 'Be more concerned with your character than your reputation, because your character is what you really are, while your reputation is merely what others think you are'.

Brilliance starts with you choosing to own who you are and giving yourself permission to live and lead from this space. Faking it till you make it is not a strategy for becoming more brilliant. Hope, or hoping to become more brilliant, isn't a strategy either.

How can you teach, guide, mentor and lead others if you aren't being the best version of yourself?

How can you give to others when you're not giving to yourself?

You are the strategy.

You are the key to change.

Better is something you become

Sir Edmund Hillary, the first confirmed climber to reach the summit of Mount Everest, said 'It's not the mountain we conquer, but ourselves'.

Absolutely! We must conquer our own limitations! We have to get curious about the imperfections that are holding us back and explore how we can move forward. We have to be prepared to disrupt the present to create a new future. We have to explore the road less travelled, to embrace questioning and explore the possibilities of what could be.

Those who are truly unleashing their brilliance have an insatiable desire and commitment to develop, to learn, to become better and more brilliant, every day.

Stepping out of the safety of what you know and where you're sitting comfortably right now is scary as hell! It often means big ups and downs — a rollercoaster rather than a gentle turn on a merry-go-round. That can be extremely confronting.

Yet in business, and in life, there's no free ride. It's the people who are willing to challenge themselves — to make themselves accountable for their own success and happiness, who engage with others, who recognise the need to reach that little bit further — who end up more successful, satisfied and happy.

Decide today that better is something you will become — set this as an intention.

Decide right now: what is one thing you're going to do differently today to take you into tomorrow?

Lessons from Mildred

'We've all got these voices in our heads telling us we can't do something or not to do it, sabotaging our success,' explained Sherilyn Shackell, Founder and Global CEO of The Marketing Academy, in Episode 022 of my podcast, *Unleashing Brilliance*. 'Well I've characterised mine: an orangutan called Mildred. Whenever I hear this voice on my shoulder, I can say "Shut up, Mildred. You're a bloody orangutan. You're not serving me"'.

Yes, I too laughed out loud when Sherilyn shared this with me! She is so right, I thought. I can't believe how many times the voices in my own head have told me that I'm not good enough, I can't do something until I've done something else or I'll look stupid and people will laugh at me. We all have these crazy voices in our heads. We just don't all call them Mildred the orangutan — though maybe we should! It would help us see a different side to the story, and one we may not have to engage with.

'The voices in our heads can serve us for good, the mundane and the boring, or they can actually do us harm,' Sherilyn adds. 'This voice, Mildred, my orangutan, she is fiercely protective over me. When I walk into an environment that I can't control and I'm feeling vulnerable and I'm not sure how people are perceiving me, she's saying "Don't do that.

Don't do that thing because you are going to look like an idiot". She's trying to protect me'.

Professor Ron Heifetz from Harvard Kennedy Business School describes these inner voices as our 'internal coding' between the perceived *role* of how we think we should be and the *self* or the *who* we're challenging ourselves to become. He suggests that these lines of code are developed through time. Some are hard coded and cemented, often associated with ancestral and cultural norms. Others, he suggests, are flexible and can be renegotiated or even forgiven should we choose.

He has identified three types of voices:

1. *Professional internal voices* tell us how we should behave and operate at work because of the job we do, the title we have or the qualifications and expertise we've acquired over time.

2. *Social and familial voices* tell us what's appropriate for our role in society, or within the family, in terms of how we should be living our life and behaving accordingly.

3. *Ancestral voices* that through generations have passed down messages and internal coding about how we should be and behave, and the identity we have to have, based on cultural and ancestral norms.

Ron shares that while some of this coding works to our advantage and is perfect to hang onto, some of it no longer serves us. He invites us to identify the voices that no longer serve us and to choose to let them go or find ways to renegotiate the contract.

I'll admit, I'm rubbish at cooking and looking after the house — something that I thought I should be great at because my mum was always so awesome at these things. I do get heart palpitations when my Nigella-like friends come to visit — and don't ask me about the pile of washing that often ends up (for days) in the living room. But, for the most part, I've learned to accept the way I am and to laugh at my not-so-strong points, even if it does mean donning a safety vest on a Friday night to enter my house.

I used to listen to the social voices about what I thought a great mum had to be like. They'd fuel my guilt of being a working parent, telling me I *should* be at home, I *should* be at pick-up, I *should* be involved in every single breathing moment of my children's existence. It was only when I renegotiated the contract and gave myself permission to own the fact that I was an awesome mum, parenting in a way that was right for my family to live fulfilled and happy lives, and that it was absolutely okay to be a mum and an executive, that the guilt disappeared.

Guilt serves no purpose, nor adds any value, to anyone.

It's time to recognise the inner voices that are feeding your brilliance.

Identify also the inner voices that are restricting your growth or putting out your dreams: how could you renegotiate your contract with these voices or reframe your thinking on them? It's time to let go and move forward.

Superheroes have weird flaws, too

Superman is crippled by Kryptonite, the Flash complains about the pain of running too fast, Wonder Woman would be rendered useless if her bracelets were used by others against her and Thor's powers are only enhanced when he is holding his hammer. In a nutshell, superheroes are only as strong as their weakness. It's only when they combine their strengths (and likewise their flaws) that they're able to beat evil. Yet so many of us strive to be 100 per cent perfect, to be the superhero of 'me'.

We work hard to hide our imperfections, hoping that our weaknesses and the things we don't like about ourselves will somehow magically disappear. We invest, and invest, and invest even more, looking for the one-hit miracle cure or seven easy steps to master whatever it is we're trying to master. And while continual learning and personal development are an important part of growth, there's no one-stop-shop external solution to something that's sometimes part of our intrinsic being.

We all have our Kryptonite. We can no longer try and outrun this or ignore that, because it's unsustainable and exhausting! Sooner or later the fact that we're human will reveal itself!

And don't just take my word for it: Sylvester Stallone only had bit-parts in films until he scored the part of the underdog in *Rocky*; Bill Gates's first company, Traf-O-Data, failed miserably, but the learning spawned a multibillion giant; Bethany Hamilton had her arm bitten off by a shark but was back on her surfboard one month later, and two years after that, she won first place in the Explorer Women's Division of the NSSA National Championships; Richard Branson has dyslexia but instead of giving up, he embraced the power of his personality to drive him to success.

Identify your blind spots. Become comfortable with them. Accept they don't have to hold you back.

Silvia Damiano is one of the world's leading neuroleadership specialists and creator of the i4 Neuroleader Program, Model & Methodology as well as award-winning director of the documentary *Make Me a Leader*. When I asked Silvia for her thoughts on owning our flaws she shared, 'I notice that leaders today are becoming increasingly stressed, scattered, moody and anxious and this affects how well they are able to listen to others, manage their emotions and make decisions. Understanding our blind spots (flaws) helps us become more self-aware. And with self-awareness we recognise what's important to us. It helps us display behaviours that match what we value'. She adds, 'We can start to understand that both strengths and limitations are part of our human makeup and feeling "one" rather than "fragmented" is at the core of authenticity'.

I equally love American investor Chris Sacca's description of flaws, which he describes as our unique weirdness. He says, 'Weirdness is what sets us apart, gets us hired. Be your unapologetically weird self. In fact, being weird may even find you the ultimate happiness'.

Being brilliant is a practice that requires you to embrace the good, the bad, the ugly and the weirdness of you.

So, what flaws, or blind spots, do you currently have that you can embrace and accept as being part of your perfectly imperfect self?

Take off the itchy jacket

Rather than seeking and searching, let's hit the pause button for a moment and take some time to reflect on the values that we have, because that's where the answers lie.

As Brené Brown said in her fabulous book *The Gifts of Imperfection*, 'Owning our story can be hard, but not nearly as difficult as spending our lives running from it'.

Your values, like a guiding light, are the things that are important to you, that will drive you and feed the powerful connections and support around you. They will be the behaviours within which you thrive, where you will move faster and become better.

In his book *Legacy*, James Kerr writes, 'Authenticity allows us to author our own lives, to make our own original imprint and to write our own story in a voice that is true to our values'.

However, when we're not living our values, we feel like we're wearing an itchy jacket. We'll try and try to shrug off the jacket, feeling annoyed, out of kilter, uncomfortable, confused and unhappy.

If we're not careful, in our effort to chase our dreams and become our brilliant selves we can lose sight of our values, of who we are and what we stand for. We think that to be the best and to become the best, we have to behave in a certain way to fit in. (I've certainly been there, as I shared earlier.)

We may feign interest in an idea, nod in agreement when we disagree, go along with group think, laugh along with the boss's inappropriate joke or do what the client wants.

Maryam Kouchaki, organisational psychologist and Professor of Management and Organisations at Kellogg School of Management, describes these misaligned behaviours as 'surface acting'. She says, 'Staying true to yourself matters, even when it is difficult, because we notice that there is a cost involved in straying too far from your personal values'.

When do you feel like you're wearing an itchy jacket?

You are a blank canvas

In the book, *The Hungry Spirit*, Charles Handy talks about going in search of his 'white stone': a symbol for his higher self, his true character or destiny. To the outside world, Handy was successful: an oil executive, a world-renowned economist and a professor at the London Business School. But despite this external success, Handy found he was still searching for 'something'.

This year the principal of my children's secondary school decided to give each of the departing seniors a white stone. His message to them was, 'Each of you have prevailed, you have passed a number of the tests life has thrown up at you to get to where you are today. However, as you can see your names are *not* written on your white stones. Your road towards self-knowledge and self-discovery is still in its early stages. Sure, you've come a long way since when you started secondary school way back in Year 7, but your journey is only just beginning. You have an amazing opportunity to go forward and shape yourself into the person you truly want to be. Your lives are not foreordained, but instead they are a blank canvas, a white stone, on which you can create your own individual masterpieces'.

How cool is that? I share this because it applies for each of us too, not just those leaving secondary school!

There are so many different expectations that we as a society place on one another and in turn we place on ourselves: to be the fearless leader, innovative business owner, most caring friend, loving parent, passionate lover, amazing cook, incredible housekeeper...

'Toughen up. Hard work. No play. Don't show vulnerability at work. Make those tough decisions — and now,' says the *assumed* fearless leader.

'There's dust on those shelves. Get to work. Look at that pile of washing. Not good enough,' says the *assumed* incredible parent.

Yet did society set in stone these perceived rules of behaviour or is it pressure that we're unintentionally (and unnecessarily) putting on ourselves?

Falling into the trap of pleasing others, conforming to societal ideals and being all things to all people can be, if nothing else, totally draining and exhausting. Society (and each of us for that matter) may well want to put us into nicely wrapped boxes with ribbons and labels, but the reality is we're all multifaceted and multitalented.

Life is not a dress rehearsal. It constantly rolls across the screen in 3D glory, no matter what. So, if you imagined yourself in an action thriller and are stuck in an extremely boring unromantic comedy, you need to get up and act out a different genre yourself.

In her autobiography, Michelle Obama writes, 'Even when it's not pretty or perfect. Even when it's more real than you want it to be. Your story is what you have, what you will always have. It is something to own'.

So rather than always searching for answers, maybe we need to press pause and reflect, taking the time to peer beneath the surface because maybe there lie the stories about who we really are. If we're not careful, we risk rushing through life from one thing to another, losing track of who we are in the chase — and yet if we take a moment to stand still, we can reconnect and choose the part we're playing.

Nobody else can do it for you. You are your own director, producer, scriptwriter and camera operator. You are quite often catering, wardrobe, hair and makeup as well.

Stop playing a supporting role in someone else's dream and start stepping into your spotlight as the lead role.

Step into your future

A couple of years ago I received the most beautiful thank you note from one of my mentoring clients. (Thank you, Emily, if you ever read this.) It said:

Our conversation earlier this year really stuck in my mind — you advised me to approach this my way, and believe it is possible to do that and to shut out the naysayers with my Jetson's bubble. It's advice I've clung to, shared and celebrated.

It was a lovely note to get in itself, but it also reinforced for me just how much power rests in each of us to create change and momentum for another: to begin a new flow in direction or reinforce a decision. You are capable of creating significant ripples of change even when you don't realise it — but only when you're being the *you*, you want to be.

When it comes down to it, you are your own biggest business asset. *You* are unique, *you* are special, *your* ideas and opinions are needed. *You* are more than enough.

Don't waste momentum looking sideways or backwards. Look straight ahead, and pump your arms into your own successful future.

Brilliance in action

1. Own your spotlight

Spend three minutes writing down or talking to someone about all the things you're good at. Own how awesome you are. Go on: put a spotlight on yourself and your brilliance.

2. Own your story

Draw a horizontal or vertical line on a piece of paper and create the timeline of you. What are some of the key events that have happened in your life? What are the major decisions or choices you've made along the way? What did you learn about yourself from these? What did these events teach you?

(continued)

Brilliance in action (*cont'd*)

3. Name the voices

Identify the voices in your head and characterise them (like Sherilyn did with Mildred the orangutan): are they professional, social or ancestral voices? Are they serving you right now? If not, why not? How can you renegotiate with them?

Look in the mirror and practise saying to your inner Mildred, 'I get it. Thank you for looking out for me and protecting me, but I'm good. I've got this'.

4. Take off the itchy jacket

When do you feel like you're wearing an itchy jacket?

Write down your top three personal values with an example of when the value was aligned. Use the table to help you. Then write down an example of when each of your values wasn't aligned or isn't aligned right now. Think about how you can make sure you live and lead more by your values.

My Personal Value	Aligned	Misaligned	Ideas for improvement
EXAMPLE: No judgement	In weekly meeting everyone is encouraged to speak up and thier voice is heard and opinions valued	My boss always comments about younger staff being lazy	Share with my boss the incredible work of the younger members of the team

Facet 2

Focus

Imagine if former sprinter and world record holder Usain Bolt ran with his head turned to the side, comparing himself to others, always watching the person in the next lane. What do you think would happen? Well, I don't think he would be known as the greatest sprinter of all time, that's for sure. I think he would be known as the man who lost focus, fell over, seriously injured himself and cursed himself for his mistakes for the rest of his life!

In the same way, so many of us get confused and distracted looking to the left and the right, in front and behind, watching what everyone else is doing, losing focus or jumping onto the 'next big thing' instead of staying in our lane. We then sit, with our head in our hands wondering why we don't seem to be moving forward. We get stuck in inaction.

How often have you found yourself going off on a tangent, only to come back a few days, weeks or months later, head hanging, kicking yourself for not thinking things through; asking yourself, 'What the hell was I thinking?' We all have to fight the desire to chase the shiny objects that pop up in our periphery.

The most successful global businesses — Google, Apple, Pixar, Amazon — have at their heart a very basic tenet. They see that in order to succeed, they need to improve against their own benchmarks, not necessarily those of their competitors.

Now I'm not saying *don't* pay attention to your competition at all, but in a world that demands more of you than ever, doesn't it make sense that your biggest competition is you?

When it comes down to it, you are your own biggest business asset. The biggest competition you have is yourself.

Like Usain Bolt and his vision of being the fastest man on earth, you need to get focused on your own gold medal because only then can you make sure to take the right steps towards your goals.

Are you so busy obsessing about what other businesses or people are doing that you're running for bronze instead of for gold?

How hungry are you?

You can have all of the determination and drive in the world, all of the passion, the vision and purpose imaginable, but unless you're able to answer the following questions with honesty, you'll always struggle to hit your goal.

- ◆ How hungry are you?

- ◆ How hungry are you *really*?

- ◆ How badly do you want to achieve your goal?

- ◆ How much are you prepared to sacrifice along the way?

How many people do you know who have said, 'I really want X or Y' and have set off with plans, roadmaps and vision boards, then four years later those plans are sitting untouched and forgotten because they weren't prepared to give their absolute heart and soul, the pulse and the heartbeat, to getting X or Y? This doesn't make them bad people, or bad leaders, or bad entrepreneurs. It accounts for 99 per cent of us who don't have that fire in the belly for whatever it is we've set out to achieve.

If you have that fire, however, you:

- take risks and accept the consequences of those risks

- zig where others zag

- invest the time that's needed without fuss or complaint

- think outside the box, and redesign, rebrand and relaunch the box

- accept (and seek out) constructive criticism from mentors

- look for outside influences

- make the most of every opportunity presented to you

- seek out chances to improve and become better every day.

Angela Duckworth talks to the concept of hunger in her TED Talk *Grit: The power of passion and perseverance*. She says,

> *Grit is passion and perseverance for very long-term goals... having stamina... sticking with your future, day-in, day-out. Not just for the week, not just for the month, but for years... working really hard to make that future a reality. Grit is living life like it's a marathon, not a sprint.*

If you have that fire within, then you will seize the day, the month, the year, the opportunity. As Napoleon Hill wrote in his all-time classic *Think and Grow Rich*, 'There is one quality which one must possess to win and that is definiteness of purpose, the knowledge of what one wants, and a burning desire to possess it'.

Cathy Burke is a brilliant example of someone with a burning desire who has never been afraid of a challenge.

Cathy is one of seven children. When I interviewed her for my podcast, Cathy talked about being the 'odd kid'. Her mother struggled with mental health and Cathy struggled with the stigma of her mother being in and out of psychiatric wards. Finally, she was able to escape to university, where she discovered punk anarchy and politics. She describes herself as a ratbag, comfortable with the unknown and playing on the edges of change.

It was a trip to Goda-Chili, Ethiopia in 1992 that changed Cathy forever. She was a young mum, and Live Aid had captured the world's attention about Ethiopia's famine. The consequences of this were visible during her visit there as a volunteer with The Hunger Project, an organisation committed to the sustainable end of world hunger.

As a young mum herself, Cathy said she couldn't imagine what other mothers go through seeing their kids die of something like a common cold or diarrhoea. 'I just had to do something about it,' she said.

Cathy promised a group of villagers that she would be their voice. Her inner fire was lit.

As she shares, 'I questioned who I was to say this when surely someone like the World Bank should be doing something. But the realisation was, just as I am a renegade Perth girl, a bit of a dag, I could still have a say in how the world goes. Digging into my own leadership and my own power to find what I needed and who I needed to be, to serve in that way, was critical'.

Cathy Burke ended up becoming CEO of The Hunger Project for 20 years. Through her work, millions of the world's poorest people have stepped into their own leadership and have been able to feed themselves and their family. According to their website, The Hunger Project has a global reach of more than 15.9 million people living in rural villages in Africa, India, Bangladesh and Latin America. Cathy's inner hunger and passion to unlock human potential, building movements to drive change, has been a consistent part of her life and now her legacy lives on.

Cathy's focus around ending world hunger fuelled her work, every decision she made, every action she took and everything that she continues to do in her work.

So, what's fuelling your hunger? There will be something that lights you up, that keeps you going, that if you dig deep and think about it, is the thing that drives your passion to do and be more. And it doesn't need to be as epic as Cathy's example. It's about you and your dreams.

For example, I'm driven by a need for freedom to do the work I love, when I want to do it and in the way I like. It's about making the right decisions that will create freedom of choice for my family and how I choose to live my life. It's a passion in life and in my work to unleash the brilliance in individuals, leaders and teams, because only when we bring brilliant people together can we create extraordinary results — and isn't this what we want for ourselves, the companies we work for and the world around us?

So again, what's fuelling your hunger?

Find this inner hunger and it will fuel your focus.

Eye on the moon

A rocket to the moon with no plotted course will just go around and around in orbit, but a rocket with a plan and a program behind it, which takes into account the prevailing conditions and the mechanics of the mission, will be set to hit its target.

In much the same way, keeping your eye on the prize is key to maintaining focus. You have to regularly check in on your plan, ask yourself how you're progressing and make the moves needed to ensure you're continually heading in the right direction. Attention to your plan drives sustained motivation.

But we often get distracted with all the external forces fighting every nanosecond of our attention *and* we distract ourselves, putting things off, placing our 'somedays' and 'tomorrows' on the 'once-we-have-achieved-XYZ' list.

Here's what I mean:

- ◆ 'When I get promoted, I will ...'
- ◆ 'When I get more money, I will ...'

- 'When I have a bigger team, I will ...'

- 'When I write the book, I will ...'

- 'When I have 1000 Instagram followers, I will...'

'... I will do the thing I really want to do once I've done all the other small things that account to nothing!'

Putting things off isn't keeping your eye on the prize; it's orbiting the moon!

This is lost focus and you risk ending up in the waiting room with all the other coulda, shoulda, wouldas.

Staying in the action zone takes determination, resilience, a hunger and a belief that what you're doing — whether in a corporate organisation or on your own — means something to you.

But how? How do you tame the tornado of ideas that constantly run through your brain, competing for attention, threatening to take you off track? How do you rein in Hurricane You?

How you choose to move through life — you controlling life, or life controlling you — is up to you. You have to take ownership of your plan, your direction, your ultimate journey, your focus.

Ask yourself:

- Why am I doing what I'm doing?

- Why am I *really* doing what I'm doing?

- How are things different because of what I'm doing?

- What is the impact I want to make?

Anchor and align

I was recently mentoring a CEO of a small production company. We were discussing their vision of building a digital business, with freedom as the key driver. We started discussing plans for the next 12 months to help them get there, and as my client started sharing the plan, it became apparent that it was misaligned to the bigger vision of creating a business that could provide the opportunity to work from anywhere. The annual plan was based on the 'norm' of a traditional agency and on what the CEO thought they 'should' be doing: winning the big clients; running in-house strategy days, workshops and programs. Achieving this plan would have resulted in a fixed work location, increased staff and overheads. It didn't sound much like the picture of freedom they had shared earlier with me.

If we don't identify our key driver, we can so easily fall into the trap of doing what is expected of us and lose focus.

Maintaining focus means having an anchor for everything you do to align with. Stephen Covey put this perfectly when he said, 'The main thing is to keep the main thing the main thing'.

One activity I do every year is to choose a word or a series of words around which to anchor and align my next 365 days. You may say 'a single word can't achieve goals for you'. And you would be correct in many ways. It's just a word or a series of words, after all. Without planning, and effort, and pure hard slog, nothing will happen. But what that word does is give me a focus. It creates something tangible because, as Patrick Rothfuss said in *The Name of the Wind*, 'As names have power, words have power. Words can light fires in the minds of men. Words can wring tears from the hardest hearts'.

Independence. Profitability. Freedom. Skyrocket. If I were to ask you to get clear on the next 12 months by sharing one, single big word — or the few words — that best describes what you're doing and why over the next year, what would it be?

My good friend Gabrielle Dolan likes to work with three words and one year she had 'Fabulous, Fit and Fifty'. Gabrielle ensured she excelled in fabulousness in everything she did and every decision she made, she embraced being 50 and celebrated accordingly and she made a commitment to improving personal fitness and wellbeing.

Everything that you say and do, the action that you take, the decisions you make, the work you say 'yes' to and the work you say 'no' to needs to align to your word(s) for the next 365 days.

I've had clients use mottos such as, 'If it's not a "hell yeah" it's a "f**k no"'; words such as 'Phoenix', 'Visible', 'Nurture', 'Harvest'; and others that use an inspirational quote or meme as their anchor.

One year my word was 'Braveheart'. This meant being braver in every decision I made, stepping out courageously, saying 'yes' to things that scared me, and having a focused intent on seeing the best in people around me and being fair without judgement.

So, think about it now. What would your word(s) be to sum up your focus for the next 12 months?

How will this/these word(s) help you to stick to the things that matter?

What intentional behaviours are needed to help you deliver to your word(s)?

Plan and prioritise

Back in my university days we were taught to build detailed one-, three- and five-year plans. While I appreciate this approach may still be necessary depending on the size and scale of your organisation, the reality is this ever-changing world we're all operating in is forcing us to become more agile, adopt 90-day sprints and drive faster decision making.

Hence, it's better to nail the bigger vision, the ultimate *why*, to set the course and direction and *then* develop the plan for that next 12 months or 90 days. Focus on doing the right things and taking the right actions that will *contribute* to the bigger vision. As Jim Collins said in *Good to Great*, 'If you have more than three priorities, you don't have any'.

Prioritising isn't always easy—particularly given the scale of options and opportunities available to us right now (remember the choice fatigue I discussed previously?). But it's what we say 'no' to that contributes to our bigger vision. The late Steve Jobs explained at Apple's 1997 Worldwide Developers Conference, 'You've got to say "no, no, no" and when you say "no", you piss off people'. To Jobs, focus wasn't about willpower. It was about the courage to abandon 1000 great ideas to meet one big goal — even if that upset people in the process.

Focus takes effort, and a plan with priorities helps you pay attention and maintain focus on the right actions.

A planning exercise I run through with my clients and that I recommend you try is:

1. Grab a sheet of paper and put your anchor word(s) from before at the top.

2. Identify key projects for the next 12 months that are going to contribute to achieving that/those word(s).

3. Break it down further: thinking about your 12 months as four quarters, commit to one or two projects per quarter that would get you closer to that goal.

4. Think about what you need to do to achieve those projects — for example, this book didn't write itself. I had to plan a quarter of research and planning time, a quarter of writing and editing time, a quarter of marketing planning and a quarter of go-to market strategy. Without breaking a project into realistic and sizeable chunks it won't get finished.

As the old saying goes: eat the elephant one bite at a time.

Quit looking in the rear-view mirror

In early 2013, Extended Stay America, a national hotel chain, was coming back from the brink of bankruptcy. Staff were afraid to stick their necks out, make decisions or disrupt the status quo in any way, whether it was being afraid to give an unhappy guest a free night's accommodation or make decisions about a property. Why? Because they were fully aware of financial pressures and potential layoffs and, as a result, they were too nervous to show any of their own bravery. Despite being part of a bigger team, individually they felt alone.

Jim Donald, the CEO, decided that spending too much time looking in the rear-view mirror wasn't going to solve anything. He knew the answers were in front of him, that his team were capable of playing an integral part in the turnaround — if he could only encourage them to be that little bit braver. They simply had to start looking forward, trusting themselves and the network of people around them, slow down, engage, initiate ideas and take action to build a different future.

Jim created a 'safety net' in the form of miniature 'Get out of jail for free' cards, which he gave to each of his 9000 employees. In return for taking a risk on behalf of the company, all they had to do was hand the cards in — no questions asked. And the cards were used. According to reports, one manager in New Jersey cold-called a movie-production company when she heard it would be filming in the area. The film crew ended up booking $250 000 in accommodation at the hotel.

Now, this idea seemed to involve a lot of risk. What if they failed? Or worse, what if it had ended up costing the company *more* not less? Well, the company had already been in the worst possible position, and employees were stagnating. Jim Donald acted with honesty, acknowledging that failure is a part of progress and he knew that unless they stepped forward with a focused effort nothing would change.

What we do know from reading stories of amazing entrepreneurs, CEOs and thought leaders like Jim Donald is that there's one thing that separates them from the masses: it's a tipping point that takes them from zero to hero. It's the ability and willingness to take action; it's about being brave enough to courageously move forward in the right direction, versus continually looking in the rear-view mirror questioning what you should be doing better.

Forward action is what moves you from zero to hero.

What do you need to do to stop gazing in the rear-view mirror and instead look out the windscreen in front?

What would you do tomorrow if you had your own 'Get out of jail for free' card?

Grab the world by your lapels

In March 2019, I sold the LBDGroup, which I had founded and nurtured over the previous eight years. The 12 months prior to the sale I went through a lot of soul-searching: Who was I? Who did I want to become? What did I want to keep doing in my work? How was I tracking in terms of my bigger vision for myself and my family? How did my business, in its current form, fit with my vision for the next 10 years?

You have to be willing to change if you want things to change. This means you have to do things differently.

Sometimes doing things differently may mean doing the opposite of what you, or others, think you should do.

This takes a hell of a lot of bravery. You have to weigh up opportunity costs, gain a greater perspective on the direction you're heading, open your eyes to possibilities and pitfalls and ultimately be brave enough to make the decision that's right for you.

And sometimes, this may even mean slowing down to go fast. It may mean you need perspective. It may mean a hit in revenue as you change strategy. It may result in a loss of clients as you stop some product lines and launch new lines. It may even mean an increase in costs as you make investments in people, processes and platforms to drive the change.

Sometimes this is what we have to do. We have to get back to who we are and what we want to do and reset, refocus and re-align. This is the risk and the opportunity of becoming your brilliant self.

During my soul searching and strategising, I knew that for the LBDGroup to grow and evolve to its next stage it required a renewed energy and vision, a continued commitment to growth and elevation and, from a business perspective, this required all the investment that is needed to drive growth.

I also knew deep down that I wanted time to write this book; travel globally with my speaking and training work; and focus and work more closely with my inner circle of private and corporate clients.

I made a decision to re-engineer my work, selling the LBDGroup to ensure continued legacy building and impact under the new guidance, energy and focus of Paula Kensington. I'm so inspired by Paula's passion, focus and momentum behind the brand and it's wonderful to support her work.

At the time it was a risk to move away from everything that I had built over the previous eight years — all the certainty and security — and some people around me didn't understand why I was doing this. But change was necessary.

If you want to do things differently, challenge the norm, play a bigger game, ask for a pay rise or reset work boundaries, it can take risk and maybe even a hell of a lot of bravery.

It takes a level of self-belief to challenge the traditional, the 'it's always been like that' or even 'this is how I've always done it'.

It takes a willingness to try, to test, to learn and to fail.

- ◆ We have to be willing to fail — because this is bravery.
- ◆ We have to be willing to share what we know — because this is bravery.
- ◆ We have to step into our spotlight — because this is bravery.

- ◆ We have to try different ways of doing and working — because this is bravery.

- ◆ We have to manage ourselves, our boundaries, our decisions, our plans and our focus — because this is bravery.

Linda Sapadin, psychologist and author of *Master Your Fears,* says, 'Courage is taking action despite the fear'. She adds, 'You really need to be able to get beyond the fear to make your business happen'.

Maya Angelou put it like this: 'I love to see a young girl go out and grab the world by the lapels. Life's a bitch. You've got to go out and kick ass'.

Go on, get out there and kick some arse because you never know what change it can create.

Success is a series of steps

Success is not a goal. More so it is about getting clear on what success, as a series of steps, means for you. Getting clear on the projects that matter for you — keeping focused with one big word or a series of words; reclaiming time — and what you do with this will give you the focus to position yourself with impact.

Of course, there will be challenges along the way; things will not always go as planned and there will be failures. But what matters is how you face these challenges. Do you face them head on, learn from them and move forward, or do you get knocked down and stay there, always thinking, coulda, shoulda, woulda?

Brazilian lyricist and novelist Paulo Coelho says, 'Whenever you want to achieve something, keep your eyes open, concentrate and make sure you know exactly what it is you want. No one can hit their target with their eyes closed'.

Hold yourself accountable and own the highs and the lows, the results and the failures. Own the opportunity to continually learn and grow. Own your success.

Brilliance in action

1. Set your gold medal standard

What is your definition of success? What would three definitions of personal success and three of professional success be for you?

My 3 definitions of PERSONAL success are:	My 3 definitions of PROFESSIONAL success are:
1	
2	
3	

2. Choose a word to anchor and align your next 365 days

Thinking about the next 12 months, what word or series of words could you adopt as the anchor for your year? Take a moment to think deeper: what do these words mean to you in terms of how you will live, lead and make decisions?

3. Plan You

Thinking about point 2 above, make a list of the projects that matter to you over the next 365 days, how they contribute to your 'word' and why. Think about this in terms of work goals, financial goals, family goals and maybe even add in some 'just for me' goals.

How many have you got? Remember there are only 52 weeks in one year; that's 52 Saturdays and four quarters without excluding holidays or other commitments. So, be realistic... what's really critical? I mean it. What's really, really critical for you to do to get close to achieving your word?

Facet 3

Expertise

Have you ever walked into a room, looked around and then thought, 'Oh God, I'm not dressed right', 'I don't fit in', 'Ground, swallow me up now because I just don't belong here', or even 'How will I compete with *that*?'

That's exactly how Stephen Scheeler felt on his first day at Facebook as the CEO for Australia and New Zealand. He was surrounded by people who were, on average, 20 years younger than him, including founder Mark Zuckerberg. There were also some very wealthy people around him who had been there since the start of the company and were seen as cultural icons — the pillars of the brand, he told me during an interview in March 2019. He explained further, 'These people had a certain aura about them. There was this virtuous circle of great people coming in who just became even greater'.

Somehow, he had to work out how to add even *more* value to the company and in a way that he would be respected with these people who were now his peers and team. As he shared, 'You can't fall back on your resume or "kids, I'm going to tell you how it is" — this was not going to work'.

So instead, Stephen's strategy was to turn everyone around him into his teachers. He started off with honesty, telling the team, 'I really don't care if we succeed or fail and I don't care if I get fired. I'm not clinging to this job. I can get another. What I care about is you and you being successful'. He encouraged his team to move from being listeners, and sometimes unwilling ones, into teachers, admitting that he needed them to teach him how Facebook worked, how it should work, who does what and asking them for advice on what he needed to deliver on his mission.

This, he says, built credibility and understanding that he was willing to be one of them. 'Over time, my experience and wisdom was respected by the team,' he says.

> ## We all have expertise to share, irrespective of age, tenure, education, cultural background or experience.

Imagine the possibilities if we could actively turn everyone around us into our teachers, empowering them to share their wisdom with us.

Equally, imagine the opportunities that could be unlocked if we could also embrace being a teacher for others, sharing our own expertise and wisdom with confidence, knowing that it's the mutual exchange of value and smarts that will drive innovation, ideation, problem solving and ultimately momentum for each other.

Own your inner genius

In the book *Outliers*, author Malcolm Gladwell says that it takes 10 000 hours of practice to achieve mastery or expertise in a field. He cites examples such as Bill Gates, who used to sneak out of his parents' house at night to code at his high school; and The Beatles, who played over 1200 times in four short years in Germany before they launched into the United States.

It doesn't matter if you agree or disagree with Gladwell's theory, the point is that every one of you is an expert at something because you've built up time and hours 'practising'. You practise through the acquisition of skills, qualifications, study, knowledge, on-the-job experience, conversations you're part of, the work you do well and the work you suck at. Your 10 000 hours are unique to you.

You've got a certain set of skills, knowledge and experience that makes you an asset.

Have you heard of The Picasso Principle? It's based on a story about a woman who approached Pablo Picasso and asked him to draw a sketch. Picasso sketched it and gave it back to her saying, 'That will cost you $10 000'.

'But you took just five minutes to do the sketch,' she said.

'The sketch may have taken me five minutes, but the learning took me 30 years,' Picasso retorted.

You're an expert in something that's taken a level of investment to become great at. You may be a digital marketing expert, a wordsmith, a philanthropist with a big purpose, or an expert at branding who is looking to connect, collaborate and contribute to build mutual success. Equally you may be a skilled graduate looking for a new job, or a CEO looking for a board position or seeking help to navigate the complexities of global expansion.

You've worked hard to get to where you are. You've invested your time, energy and money to understand and master what you do. Until you own and share your expertise it's an uphill struggle to leverage your personal value, build engagement, or maximise connections or conversations because you'll never be able to share yourself wholeheartedly with conviction and make the impact you want to make.

Natasha Pincus is a talented, creative and internationally renowned storyteller who created the music video for Gotye's, 'Somebody That I Used to Know', which has been viewed by over half a billion people around the world (that's a lot of eyeballs!). She is also the author of *I Am Not a Genius, and So Are You*, in which she poses the question, 'What would happen to you if you were suddenly told that you are a *genius*?'

Think about this for a moment... how would being told you're a *genius* affect your self-confidence, your behaviour, your conversations and the decisions you make?

Would you be more willing and able to own and share what you know with others?

I think you would, and so I'm giving you permission right now: you are a genius! So, stop and reflect right now. Channel your inner Picasso, your inner genius.

Get clear on:

- What are you known for?

- Who do you help or serve?

- What are the problems you're solving for them?

- Why does what you do matter?

Be a flamingo

Steve Jobs once said, 'Apple really beats to a different drummer. I used to say that Apple should be the Sony of this business, but in reality, I think Apple should be the Apple of this business.'

The problem is that too many of us are either hiding or choosing to blend in, versus standing out. We're not willing to 'expose' our ability or expertise out of fear: fear of failure, fear of rejection, fear of being 'different'. (Remember Stephen Scheeler's story.)

> **In this decade of disruption there's a great blanding of the marketplace, so if you want to get ahead you need to be visible — you need to be a flamingo.**

Someone once said to me that not only does a flamingo always look amazing, it can even be so while standing on one leg!

Currently we see many businesses and people all competing on 'same': same products, services and offerings. They look and act the same, market themselves the same, and often the only differentiator ends up being price. In our effort to fit in, we're at risk of only being able to compete on price. Becoming too vanilla and looking just like everyone else, we become invisible, lost and plain old boring.

There's no impact in generic. You need to be brave enough to share your expertise, to be a flamingo in a flock of pigeons — you need to stand out as who you are, to own your story, to live by your values and to share your expertise so that we get to know you and how you can help us.

As Dr Seuss said, 'Why fit in when you were born to stand out?'

Fly your flag

Growing up in the north of England in the Thatcher years and the English stiff-upper-lip class system, I was always told that my work should speak for itself. I was told that I should be really humble, keep quiet about the things I was achieving and whatever I did, 'Janine, keep your head down and do not in any way call attention to yourself'.

The result for me, as it is for many others, is that I became invisible as I languished behind the scenes, taking a back seat and not getting noticed. I wasn't brave enough to speak up, to step into the spotlight or to stand out in any way, and in those early years it meant I was overlooked for promotions or opportunities.

I can remember a few years ago being in a training room with my good friend, seven-time world-champion surfer and chair of Surfing Australia, Layne Beachley AO. (See how easy it is to talk about others' achievements but not our own?) She was congratulating me on some work, and I responded, 'Oh, it's nothing' and tried to change the subject because that's something that I was taught to do in an effort to be humble.

Wow, I will never forget the roasting Layne gave me! 'What right do you have, Janine, not to let others see and appreciate what you do? When you ignore the compliment, it makes me want to stop encouraging you and sharing the impact you are making.'

She went on to explain to me that I was actually doing others a *disservice* by not taking compliments. I needed to embrace the thanks around the positive impact of my work because this in itself creates a multiplier effect of energy and momentum. Instead of being dismissive and going into hiding, I had to learn to embrace visibility and congratulatory feedback and share more to allow others to access my work.

And Layne is right! Are you hiding your expertise like a squirrel hoards nuts? What about keeping your thoughts, ideas and wisdom all to yourself hoping that someday someone may just by accident somehow stumble over you and do the job of bringing what you do to the world? Are you scared of sharing your thoughts, concerned about what someone may say or, even worse, that they may steal from you to use your ideas for themselves?

Your visibility will:

♦ build your reputation as an authority in your area of expertise

♦ enhance your thinking as there's nothing that crafts a message more than having to share it

♦ cement your profile as someone who is willing to give and share their thoughts, musings and ideas

♦ create a need in others to include you in their work.

You need to stop hiding in the wings, and step into your spotlight.

On a scale of 1 to 10, where 1 is terrible and 10 is brilliant, rate how well you are flying your flag right now.

It starts with *you*

For the past few years I've been working with a global property firm to elevate the numbers of women in leadership. We challenge individuals to put themselves in the spotlight, to share openly who they are, what they do and how they're a critical part of the business through the problems they solve.

Every single time fear kicks in at the start of the program — fear of speaking, of being the centre of attention, of sharing their thinking, of putting themselves out there, of being heard.

But after lots of coaching and support, they push past their fears as their confidence increases, and I see individuals shining more brightly than ever before. The realisation that they *do* have something to share that others want to hear and are interested in is incredible.

I recently read Marie Forleo's book, *Everything Is Figureoutable*, and I loved her story around trying to work out what it was she wanted to do with her life. She wrote that after reading an article about coaching, something inside her lit up. 'A deep, gentle presence inside me said, "This is who you are, this is who you're meant to be."' This knowing was swiftly followed by 'Marie, you're twenty-frickin'-three years old. Who in their right mind is ever going to hire a twenty-three-year-old life coach?'

Marie Forleo has gone on to host the award-winning show *MarieTV*, has millions of fans listening to her podcast, runs the business training program B-School and was named by Oprah Winfrey as a thought leader for the next generation. Now imagine if she had listened to that inner voice telling her 'Who are you to say that?'

Staying invisible is the antithesis of owning your spotlight — in fact, it's not brilliant at all.

The need to stand out in your market has never been stronger than it is today. We're bombarded with more information than we can cope with and we're bogged down in processing data, so much so that we're becoming desensitised or trying desperately to make sense of what's relevant and true. And amid all this noise *you* have to stand out, be noticed and be seen as relevant to build your career or your business: to lead a life of influence.

Being able to add value to those around you — your clients, customers, team and suppliers — is critical to being in demand. Your confidence to share your opinions, thinking and ideas will help you lead your area of responsibility, company or industry.

Lewis Howes is a former athlete and professional football player. He is now the host of the podcast *School of Greatness*, which has had over 400 million downloads since its launch in 2013. He said, 'Each day you're presented with a choice. You can either keep your greatness hidden under a pile of fears, regrets, and excuses, or you can let it out.' He advises that we need to make a conscious effort to live every single day as the best versions of ourselves, and I couldn't agree more.

Here are four ways, right now, you can magnify your own expertise:

1. *Speak.* Share that idea you have. Market that product you have. Take the lead at meetings and focus on embracing diversity of opinion, a productive use of time and generating key outcomes and actions. Offer to speak at client conferences or industry events to raise your personal profile.

2. *Contribute.* Get involved in discussions, take part in forums and get more involved in a community around your area of expertise. Participate. Contribute. Get noticed for being you and for what you think.

3. *Publish.* Write that book, article or blog you want to write. Let others access your thinking.

4. *Share.* Share your expertise, feedback and encouragement unconditionally with others. Acknowledge awesomeness in others; celebrate their successes and achievements. Encourage others more.

Don't be afraid to be seen, to speak out and to contribute your expertise. It's this that changes the world.

Share your greatness

Gabrielle Dolan is a thought leader in storytelling, working with thousands of individuals and leaders across the globe teaching them the importance of telling stories to share their expertise, values and messages. She explains, 'Besides communicating their message, personal stories also have hidden benefits. Every time someone shares a personal story it reveals something about themselves. About their family, about their upbringing, about their interests about their fears, about their values ... and this can fast track and strengthen relationships'.

She goes on to say, 'Ironically, stories about when you have not lived the values and the regret you have or the lesson you learnt, demonstrate the importance of that value even more. These types of stories that show vulnerability, can have the greatest influence'.

Sharing your story creates memorability, embeds learning and drives influence. Your story helps us understand your character — who you are, what you stand for and why you do what you do — which helps to enhance your positioning in your marketplace and builds an appreciation of your expertise.

Consumers want to know the depth behind the logo, the thinking, story and rationale behind the brand, behind you. They want to know that they and their business matter. And they want to learn from you and also from your mistakes!

Think about sharing stories through:

- presentations
- articles and blogs
- coaching and mentoring.

What more could you do tomorrow to share stories and shine the spotlight on what you're doing and the impact you're making?

Brilliance in action

1. Channel your inner genius

Answer these questions:

- What are you known for?

- Who do you help or serve?

- What are the top three problems you're solving for them?

- Why does what you do matter?

2. Be a flamingo

What makes you different and unique? What really makes you, you? Is it your experience to date? The number of companies and industries you've worked in? Maybe it's the fact you're a trained fashion designer and now working in IT development or that you've lived and worked all over the world. Your experience is your uniqueness. Think about it. Get clear and be that flamingo.

3. Fly your flag

How well are you sharing what it is that you do right now? How visible are you really? Rate yourself out of 10, where 1 is invisible and 10 is visible.

What did you notice?

There are always things we can improve on. What ideas have you got for flying your flag more?

How can I fly my flag:

- Speak more?

- Contribute more?

- Publish more?

- Share more?

Watch out!

Now that we know what we have to work towards, we also need to be aware that there are internal forces working *against us*. These shadows creep up on us when we least expect it and work tirelessly to prevent us from owning our spotlight.

These are the antitheses of Law 1:

1. Self-doubt

2. Fear of being different

3. Fear of failure

4. Tall poppy syndrome

5. Resistance to change

Let's explore them.

1. Self-doubt

Are we ever good enough? Like, really?

It's like we have a pet gremlin living inside our heads, feeding on our inner dialogue:

◆ 'Are you sure you can do this?'

◆ 'Do you think you're good enough?'

◆ 'What if you fail?'

◆ 'What's everyone else doing?'

I've lost track of how many times these questions come up in my training and mentoring work. Even after the immediate rush of achieving that promotion, winning that sale or finally making that decision, it doesn't take long for the self-doubt or feelings of punching above your weight to kick in.

The worry of whether you can do it.

The concern around whether you can make it.

The question around whether you made the right decision.

Entrepreneur and Global CEO of Business Chicks, Emma Isaacs, shared with me on my podcast, 'There's never a day that passes when I don't doubt myself in some capacity'.

Self-doubt is exhausting, and it gets in the way of real progress.

The curated content found every day on social media certainly doesn't help. We're bombarded with opportunities to compare and contrast our lives with the lives of others. We're so busy observing what everyone else is doing that we start feeling completely inadequate. (More on that in a moment.)

These feelings of self-doubt are also often referred to as 'imposter syndrome'. This term was first coined in 1978 by two American psychologists, Pauline Clance and Suzanne Imes. They described it as a feeling of 'phoniness in people who believe that they are not intelligent, capable or creative despite evidence of high achievement'. They added that while these people 'are highly motivated to achieve', they also 'live in fear of being "found out" or exposed as frauds'.

In the *Harvard Business Review* article 'Overcoming imposter syndrome', author Gill Corkindale shares that, 'Imposters suffer from chronic self-doubt and a sense of intellectual fraudulence that override any feelings of success or external proof of their competence. They seem unable to internalise their accomplishments, however successful they are in their field'.

You know exactly what I'm talking about!

You're about to give a presentation on a proposal you've been working on for months and you worry about messing it up; you get that promotion and immediately start thinking about the people you were up against and questioning your ability to do the job; you decide to take action A instead of B and then spend way too long going around in circles questioning your decision.

Quit the negative self-talk. Stop focusing on what others are doing and achieving. This is your race to run.

2. Fear of being different

Rick Barry is an American retired professional basketball player who played in both the American Basketball Association (ABA) and National Basketball Association (NBA). Barry was known for an unorthodox free-throw technique called the underhanded free throw (aka the 'granny shot'). His success with the granny shot made him one of the best free-throw shooters of all time.

Playing this shot involves holding the sides of the ball firmly with both hands, bending your knees and lifting both arms at the same time before releasing the ball smoothly. The use of fewer moving parts (such as elbows and wrists) supposedly results in a more perfect arc. Barry insists that it's accurate.

He holds a free-throw average of 90 per cent. Compare this to LeBron James, regarded by some as the greatest player of all time, who scored only 74.4 per cent of his attempts from the line while the NBA's league average has hovered north of 75 per cent ever since 2001–02.

But players hardly ever use the granny shot — in fact, there appears to be an aversion to even trying the technique.

Many players who have tried this shot stopped playing it because they were teased or felt it looked silly, in some cases despite the fact that their free-throw shots were better when taken as granny shots.

So, despite there being a potentially more brilliant way to shoot, the stigma that comes with the granny shot makes the majority of players choose the overhand throw, which actually minimises the opportunity for success.

When I asked my 16-year-old son about this, he said, 'No-one shoots like that, Mum. You'd look stupid'.

There's no doubt that being the same as everyone else is a comfortable place to be. It's great to feel like we belong. Yet when we do this, we're unconsciously choosing to stay the same. Despite sometimes knowing or believing deep down that we could do more, we choose not to because of social convention.

Are you spending too much time trying to fit in, doing what everyone else is doing? Is this need to conform actually eroding your individuality and the uniqueness that ultimately allows you to stand out?

3. Fear of failure

It's understandable to feel paralysed with fear when doing something life-threatening, like walking the cliff-hanging edge of Crib Goch — 923 metres above sea level — in Snowdonia, Wales. (That was me many years ago.)

'Fear is a fundamental part of human psychology. Our brains are wired to feel fear because it helps us avoid a calamity; it keeps us safe,' says Deep Patel on Entrepreneur.com.

The fear response starts in a region of the brain called the amygdala, which activates our fight-or-flight mode as well as triggering the release of stress hormones and the sympathetic nervous system. The role of the amygdala is to prepare us to be more efficient when in danger: the brain becomes alert, breathing accelerates, heart rate and blood pressure rise. A part of the brain called the hippocampus is closely connected with the amygdala. The hippocampus and prefrontal cortex help the brain interpret the perceived threat to determine whether the threat is real or not.

But many of us are crippled by fear on a daily basis, even when events aren't actually life-threatening.

I'm sure there are few businesspeople who have gone through their careers without experiencing fear: loss of face, loss of market share, loss of revenue, loss of job, or worse still, loss of forward momentum. Many question, 'Can I?', 'Who would want to listen to me?', 'Do I have the experience to do this?'

The truth is that fear is present every day. The difference is that some of us choose to listen to it and others embrace it.

Do you choose fear and inaction, or do you choose to turn fear into a powerful tool for success?

As Eleanor Roosevelt said, 'You gain strength, courage and confidence by every experience in which you really stop to look fear in the face ... you must do the thing which you think you cannot do'.

The fear of looking stupid, failing, not having enough money, losing a sale, forgetting our words — whatever it may be — stops us from moving forward.

You've got to face fear head-on, honouring and thanking it for looking out for you. Explore all the options while breathing deeply, trusting yourself and turning negative thoughts into positive ones.

Take a moment to list up to five things you're fearful of and ask yourself 'why?' Try to challenge these assumptions and get curious about what opportunity could exist if you didn't fear the fear.

4. Tall poppy syndrome

The Urban Dictionary defines tall poppy syndrome as Australian slang for the tendency to criticise highly successful people (i.e. tall poppies) and 'cut them down'.

This term is so ingrained in our unconscious that too many of us are afraid to share our success, to talk about what we're bringing to the table, to highlight our strengths.

As part of the networking events at the LBDGroup, we asked guests to share one thing they're high-fiving or celebrating as a win from the last month. It's incredible how challenging this can be for some people.

We don't support, celebrate and nurture those individuals enough who had a dream and followed it with personal commitment, resilience, determination and focus — even though they may have made a lot of sacrifices to achieve their dreams.

Why is it that we're inclined to cut the tall poppy off at the knees?

I personally experienced the tall poppy syndrome when I first arrived in Australia. After working damn hard in the UK through university, landing my dream job and climbing the corporate ladder to achieve senior management status under 30, I found it really tough to get a job. I sought advice from a consultant, whose response was 'wear pink and pretend you don't know the answer even if you do!'

Needless to say, this was not advice I followed.

I think it's time we embraced and celebrated the tall poppy. I think it's time we admired the success of those who have achieved more than the average person. I think it's time, through our actions and words, to present the gold medal to those individuals taking ownership of their own business and career success and achieving their dreams.

And above all, I think it's well and truly time for each of us to celebrate and high-five our own successes, achievements and strengths.

List the top three things you want to give yourself a high five for this month. Why not make this a habit and make an appointment with yourself every month to reflect on your achievements? Or even better: find an accountability buddy and make this part of your monthly commitment to each other.

5. *Resistance to change*

The flipside of this is that many of us can end up operating with our blinkers on. We get *so* stuck and *so* focused on an end goal that we miss seeing other opportunities. Or, we become resistant to change, believing that our way is the only way, thinking we know everything — stuck in our siloed thinking, unwilling to learn and listen to well-meaning advice.

And so we risk:

◆ losing customers and clients to other more relevant brands

◆ failing to attract, recruit and retain talent due to the unattractiveness of our offering

- competing with new players entering the market and challenging our products and services

- churning through the day making small adjustments and readjustments in the hope that these small actions will spark significant momentum — but of course, it's a mere blip.

The real risk is that we become irrelevant and invisible as the world and market continue to move and evolve around us. Staying stuck in our ways ultimately ends in a self-propagating disaster heading in one direction: down a slippery slope to failure.

So, think about where you're at right now and what you could do to create forward momentum and change.

Take the blindfold off and jump!

Law 2: Be Ready

Harness your energy

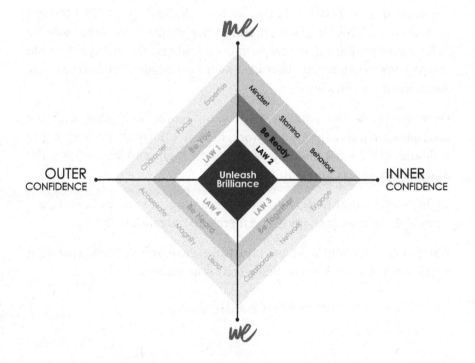

Take back control.
Stop the busy — it's an excuse.
Fuel your energy and bring your best.

If I were to ask 'How are you?', what are the chances your first response would be 'busy'?

Every person I speak to, everywhere I go, is running around like a maniac, meeting to meeting, email to email, with a diary packed to the hilt. We have so many to-do lists it is impossible to think about what's for lunch, let alone about what's next. Once we throw in some time for looking after ourselves, keeping fit, eating well, getting enough sleep and squeezing in hugs for the important people in our world, it's no wonder we feel like we're living — no, just *existing* — in Crazy Town.

Many of my clients are well and truly '[skidding] in broadside in a cloud of smoke, thoroughly used up, totally worn out', as Hunter S Thompson wrote. Although they're not shouting 'Wow! What a ride!' but rather riding through a shit storm, stuck on a rollercoaster, not knowing which way is up, down, left, right or any direction at all.

Yet while we're regularly told that we have to 'dig deep', to 'find the grit and resilience' to keep going and that 'once we get to the other side we will become stronger and have so many learnings,' the reality is that life can feel downright crappy, horrible, rough (permission to insert as many swear words as you see fit).

Over the years, I've witnessed so many people struggling with the multiple demands of home and work, of Plan A not quite eventuating as it should, of the emotional ride of incredible highs and insane lows. The 21st century sure is unrelenting!

Right now, you may be agreeing and grumbling, 'It's not my fault; I can't control the demands on my diary; there's just so much to do!'

But the truth is, being 'too busy' is just an excuse. Yep, you heard me right and I'm going to say it again: being busy is an excuse.

It's an excuse for being out of control, for giving in to others' demands on our time, for not taking ownership and for lacking personal discipline. Being busy simply means saying 'yes' and committing to too many things.

Every time we make the 'busy' excuse, we deflect the responsibility for our own actions. We give our control over to others. This is not harnessing your energy — this is depleting you of every little last ounce of reserve that you have to be your brilliant self.

We have to adopt an excuse-free attitude and invite the opportunity to be time rich and thriving.

I can say this with authority because I have absolutely been there too.

My first serious trip to the world of Crazy Town was after I had my first child, Flynn. I went back to work as a full-time marketing manager when he was just five months old. My husband Jason took paternity leave and we juggled like mad. At the time I didn't feel like I had any choice: recently arrived in Australia, rebuilding my career, starting out on a reduced salary and not getting paid for maternity leave. We didn't have any family support around us as they were overseas or interstate. Add to this that Flynn was our first child, so we had absolutely no clue what we should be doing and all the while my energy levels were being gradually depleted as I attempted to do everything and be the perfect parent, manager, partner and friend.

In hindsight, this was the first time I experienced burnout and operating from a place of survival. I had no energy, a feeling of helplessness, of not having any choice — and yet I robotically got myself out of bed every morning to keep going, to respond to the commitments I had put on myself.

Until I got to the point where one day I'd had enough and said to my boss, 'I can't do this anymore. I either leave or I reduce my hours'. Strangely enough, the answer was an unexpected, 'What can we do to help?'

Being exhausted isn't leadership.

Being exhausted isn't inspiring to others.

To become your brilliant self you need to realise you are human, and you need to make some tough choices and decisions that often mean saying 'no'.

This is the focus of Law 2, Be Ready: Harness your energy, becoming masterful at taking back control, thriving energetically, kicking excuses to the kerb, ensuring that you're doing all you can to be the best version of yourself mentally, physically and spiritually every day. This is the only way to create influence and impact.

So, how are you doin'?

The only way to move forward is to understand where you're at now. To think about what's really going on and to identify change. To be *completely* honest with yourself.

Take a look at this diagram. Where do you feel you are right now in your professional life?

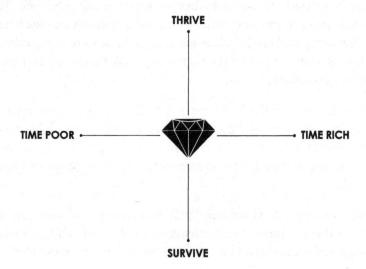

- *Surviving or thriving?* Thinking about how you're feeling right now, where would you place yourself along the axis of surviving to thriving?

  - Do you feel energised every day, ready to take on whatever comes your way, irrespective of whether it's been planned or not?

  - Or are you in survival mode doing just enough to keep life going, staying afloat, struggling to keep your head above water, or even floating behind on what you want to accomplish each day?

- *Time poor or time rich?* Now, where would you place yourself on the axis of time poor or time rich?

  - Do you find yourself with very little time to do anything? Are you well and truly a resident of Crazy Town, running around out of control and tackling whatever the most important thing seems to be at that time?

  - Or are you in control of your diary with enough time in there to do nothing with, to maybe think and percolate ideas?

Now grab a pen and draw an 'X' on the spot that you feel best represents where you're at.

What do you notice?

You may feel like you're thriving every day, doing what you truly love but the demands on your time are *insane.* You'd love to have some time to read and relax, time to take a leisurely walk or maybe just do *nothing.* Yet, the reality is your diary is so jammed with every single minute and second accounted for and if anything runs over time the chaos well and truly sets in. You're doing a lot of stuff but rarely feel like you're getting on top of things and so you find yourself placing an 'X' in the top left-hand side.

Alternatively, you may be feeling like you have all the time in the world and you're just going through the motions of life. Work or life may have hit a rut. You're a human *doing* but not necessarily a human *being*. If this is the case, you may find you place an 'X' in the bottom right-hand quadrant.

Our ultimate aim is to place ourselves in the top right-hand quadrant. A place where we're thriving as individuals, loving the things we're doing and feeling like we're doing things that matter. We want to feel like we have time to explore, to think, to be spontaneous, to take advantage of opportunities as they arise — or just to sit and breathe!

This is a place where you're truly able to harness your energy and make the difference you want to make.

The 3 facets of Law 2

In an episode of the *Lead to Win* podcast, 'Self-care as a leadership discipline', leadership expert Michael Hyatt describes self-care as 'the activities that make for a meaningful life outside of work, while contributing to better performance at work'.

Jim Loehr, co-author of *The Power of Full Engagement*, says, 'Productivity is less about managing your time and more about managing your energy'.

It doesn't matter how much you master any of the Laws in this book; without having the energy to bring the best of yourself to everything you do, you'll never achieve the brilliance that you're capable of for yourself, or be in the best position to unleash it in others. This is the essence of Law 2.

Law 2 means you must address three facets:

- ◆ Mindset
- ◆ Stamina
- ◆ Behaviour.

So that's exactly what we'll do next.

Facet 4

Mindset

In the 1940s, the record for running a mile was 4:01 minutes. But it hadn't budged for years. Some doctors and scientists said it was physically impossible to run a mile in less than four minutes. Not just hard, or dangerous, but *impossible*.

Many tried for years, but still the barrier held firm. Maybe the experts had it right? Perhaps there was a limit to what the human body could achieve.

But one man, Sir Roger Bannister, was about to prove them wrong.

In his teens, Bannister discovered he had a talent for running. He decided to train hard with the aim of getting a university scholarship, which he won, to Oxford University. While there he started getting noticed and was inspired watching the 1948 Olympics. His hard work paid off when he won a spot on the team, competing at the 1952 Olympics.

Everyone expected Bannister to win. But at the very last minute the athletics schedule changed, affecting his preparation and training routine and Bannister came in fourth.

Gutted, Bannister spent the next couple of months reflecting on his performance, questioning his 'what's next?' He thought, and he thought, and he thought. And in the end, he decided he was going to do all he could to prove himself. He was going to achieve something that hadn't been achieved before: run a mile in less than four minutes.

Bannister stepped up his training. He relentlessly visualised achieving his dream in order to create a sense of certainty in his mind and body.

On 6 May 1954, Bannister took to Oxford University's Iffley Road track. Driven by years of training and determination, Bannister crossed the finish line exhausted. He had broken the four-minute barrier, running the distance in 3:59.4 — a new record.

'However ordinary each of us may seem, we are all in some way special, and can do things that are extraordinary, perhaps until then... even thought impossible,' he said of his win.

Here's the interesting thing.

Bannister's achievement created a new belief among other athletes in what was possible. His record, which had taken years to achieve, was smashed just 46 days later by an Australian runner — even though for years the speed had never fallen below four minutes. The 'four-minute barrier' has since been broken by over 1400 male athletes. In the years since, the mile record has been lowered by almost 17 seconds, and currently stands at 3:43.13. Even strong high-schoolers today run a four-minute mile.

It took extreme certainty, a focused mind, and an inner belief for Roger Bannister to do what was considered un-doable. He alone was able to create the personal certainty and mindset without seeing any proof that it could be done. He said, 'It is the brain, not the heart or lungs, that is the critical organ'.

A focused dream + the right action = forward momentum

Bannister's achievement is an example to all of us of how often it's only our mind that's holding us back from possibility and how it only takes one person to show us what's possible for everything to completely change. Just think about it:

- Uber launched in 2010 and now there are countless rideshare services around the world.

- IBM made the first smartphone available to consumers (the Simon Personal Communicator) in 1994; 15 years later the first iPhone appeared thanks to Steve Jobs and today it's estimated that more than 5 billion people have mobile devices, and over half of these connections are smartphones.

- In 1972, Katherine Graham was the first female to be named CEO of a Fortune 500 company at the *Washington Post*. As of 1 June 2019, 33 of the companies on the ranking of highest grossing firms will be led by female CEOs for the first time ever. (Granted there is still much more work to do to lift this number!)

We often think long and hard about what we want to achieve. And if we're not thinking about the great big lightbulb moment, we're discussing it. Sometimes we think and discuss it so hard that we think and discuss ourselves right out of any action. Our thoughts and discussions impact what we believe we're capable of; the personal limitations kick in and that poor butterfly of brilliance, of self-belief, of possibility, of 'I can' is gone before it even had a chance to get its wings out of the cocoon.

Those who succeed, whose stories we sit and devour, live by a very simple set of rules. They recognise that nothing gets accomplished when we live in the abstract. Instead, they take action, with a big fat 'yes, bring it on' and 'yes, I can'.

Here's the thing: unless we have the right mindset for ourselves, we cannot possibly expect the right mindset in those around us.

Your mindset fuels the people around you: if you have belief, determination and an 'I can do this' mindset, it will cultivate the same in your team and the people around you.

Don't believe me?

Think about how amazing you feel when you're surrounded by positive people or after hearing a motivational speaker rev you up with their story of brilliance and 'you can do this too' — how their energy rubs off on you and you feel inspired and ready to leap.

Now think about bumping into Negative Nelly at the water filter or 'I'm so over this' Ian in the corridor and how their negative demeanour can affect a whole group of people, influencing them to have a similar negative attitude. As the old saying goes, 'One bad apple can spoil the bunch'.

So which mindset are you choosing: I can, or I can't?

What do you need to do differently? Why not list up to five people you need to hang around to fuel an 'I can' mindset.

Not yet, but 'I can'

I was once working with a senior female executive in a property company and during our first session she shared with me her dream: to leave Australia and work in London. When I asked her why she thought it was a dream, and not a potential reality, she cited off excuse after excuse: 'How can I, when I've got this responsibility'; 'My boss doesn't support me. He says I have to put in x number of years before I can even consider it'. Her mindset was well and truly stuck in the land of impossibility. Over our next few sessions we worked on an action plan, we visualised a future, we created a new mode of operating that included both doing and creating all — with the bigger plan in mind ... and within 12 months her dream job in London became a reality.

Examples and stories like this are everywhere: public-known stories of success as well as many in our own backyards. In my own world I've witnessed how the power of 'I can' has turned freelancers into business owners, recruiters into network creators, digital marketers into app developers, weapons engineers into business owners.

The difference between success and being brave enough to try something, failing and learning from it, comes down to focused belief and action.

Achievers have a 'can-do' mindset. They get on with it. They don't just think about it; they take action.

Stanford psychologist Carol Dweck introduced the concept of fixed and growth mindsets in her book, *Mindset*. According to Dweck, people with a fixed mindset believe that qualities such as intelligence and talent are fixed traits, so they spend their time proving these traits rather than developing them. She also contends that such people think that talent creates success without any effort needed.

Dweck says that, conversely,

> *In a growth mindset, people believe that their most basic abilities can be developed through dedication and hard work — brains and talent are just the starting point. This view creates a love of learning and a resilience that is essential for great accomplishment.*

I particularly love Dweck's take on the two words 'Not Yet'. Dweck shares the story of a school in Chicago where, as opposed to marking a course as a fail, the teacher gave students a 'Not Yet' grading. This helps create an environment where students believe that with a bit more effort and work they have the chance of getting there. 'Not Yet' fuels possibility and self-belief rather than the negative association of 'FAIL'. (Interestingly, I've heard this word being reframed as an acronym for First Attempt In Learning to try to give it a positive spin.)

So, changing our beliefs — managing out mindset — can have a powerful impact.

The growth mindset creates a powerful passion for learning, a belief that you can achieve, change things and become better. It fuels an internal fire to take ownership and move forward.

James Kerr reiterates this view in his book *Legacy*. He says,

> *where we direct our mind is where our thoughts will take us; our thoughts create an emotion; the emotion defines our behaviour; our behaviour defines our performance. So, simply, if we can control our attention, and therefore our thoughts, we can manage our emotions and enhance our performance.*

When we allow ourselves to trust in our own ideas, to follow through and act on them, we can achieve anything.

So, what limits are you putting on yourself?

How can you reframe these with your own version of 'Not Yet', or even better, 'I can'?

Befriend failure

I was once asked in an interview, 'What are you scared of?' Honestly, I'm scared of so many things — snakes, spiders, sharks, being underground — and most of all I'm scared of failure. But as opposed to this fear freezing me into inaction it's actually the one thing that has kept me going through the highs and lows. It's my motivator: it keeps me on course and focused.

It was General Colin Powell who said, 'There are no secrets to success. It is the result of preparation, hard work, and learning from failure', while Oprah Winfrey observed that 'Failing is another steppingstone to greatness'.

And yet, often our fear of failure feeds our self-doubt and before we know it our 'I can't' has suffocated any 'I can'.

Common things we say to ourselves include:

- ◆ Who would want to listen to me?
- ◆ Do I have the experience to do this?
- ◆ What if this fails?

Part of managing our mindset and becoming brilliant is an ability to acknowledge the fear and see this as an invitation to do it anyway.

To be brilliant, we have to see failure not as a dirty word but rather as an invitation to courage and an opportunity to learn how to become more. We have to be willing to fail — because this is bravery, this is courage, this is determination, this is a willingness to try and change things.

This fear of failure has been fuelled by what we learn at school, work and in the media. We're taught that failure is wrong, and that taking risk is dangerous. It has a crippling effect for many of us on a daily basis. At school, everything is either right or wrong: pass or fail. At work, performance reviews focus on our weaknesses and 360-degree reviews allow others to critique our behaviours. Media spotlights individuals' weak spots or negative stories — and, at worst, even when they are successfully achieving, they are slammed in an effort to dig up dirt and create headlines to knock them down a peg or two.

It becomes easier to 'stay safe' rather than putting ourselves out there where we risk looking stupid or being vilified.

I was reminded of this recently while listening to Jamie Pride — serial entrepreneur, venture capitalist and author of *Unicorn Tears*. In his keynote, he was discussing the fear of failure and the need to build sustainable performance through failure. He openly shared his personal failure of epic financial proportions and the impact this had on his health and wellbeing, his family and his 'what's next?'

But what struck me most was his comment about the fact that most of us are conditioned to fear failure. Yet if you look at some of the most successful individuals in play today, at some stage they have 'failed' and shown courage and strength in coming back from the edge.

The future is asking us to challenge the status quo, to disrupt thinking, to be courageous and brave, to drive change, to face our fears.

For example, Richard Branson has failed and gotten up more times than many other entrepreneurs have made a decision. He befriended failure as an invitation to keep following his dreams. While inventor Sir James Dyson, the beloved designer of the vacuum cleaner, went through 5127 prototypes and 5126 'failures' to get his phenomenally successful first model right. That's a lot of what could be termed complete and utter failure.

For me, befriending failure is facing the fear head-on, exploring all the options while breathing deeply, trusting myself, turning negative thoughts into positive and then quite simply just doing it.

If you want to do things differently, to challenge the norm or play a bigger game it takes a lot of courage. Negotiating a pay rise, resetting work boundaries, deciding to be part, or not, of a changing organisation, saying no — everything takes a lot of courage. And while it's easy to say, it's hard to do. It takes a level of self-belief to challenge the traditional: the 'it's always been like that' or even 'this is how I've always done it'.

It means going against the status quo.

Unicorns and rainbows won't happen 100 per cent of the time. So, if we're going to change anything, we have to embrace the fear, stare it in the face and say, 'I'm coming for you anyway'. We have to be willing to fail because this is bravery, this is resilience, this is grit, this is a willingness to try and change things.

What would you do differently today if instead of fearing failure you embraced it and saw it as an opportunity instead?

It takes a lot of courage to be steadfast, and it takes even more courage to befriend failure, take chances and live your dreams.

In the words of poet Erin Hanson of thepoeticunderground.com, '"What if I fall?" Oh but my darling, What if you fly?'

Brilliance in action

1. Reframe 'I can't'

We all have limitations we place on ourselves to keep us safe, but in actual fact our greatest opportunity and power lies in ourselves. Write down five 'I can'ts' and try reframing them into 'I cans'.

I can't	Actually I can
1	
2	
3	

2. Befriend failure

What could you do to celebrate failures and make them your friend? Sara Blakely of Spanx fame credits much of her success to her father, who encouraged his kids to fail. 'We'd sit around the dinner table and he'd ask, "What did you guys fail at this week?" If we had nothing to tell him, he'd be disappointed,' she said. 'He knew that many people become paralysed by the fear of failure.'

So, let's befriend failure. Why not start your own 'Failure Journal' and write a daily failure and what you learned from it? How about in your team meetings having an agenda point where the weekly failures and consequent learnings are discussed?

Facet 5

Stamina

In the case of an emergency, an oxygen mask will drop from a compartment above your head. Fit the mask to yourself first, and then assist others.

We're all pretty familiar with this instruction. We hear it every time we get onto a plane. Yet how many of us would actually adhere to this warning? I'm almost prepared to bet my life (and my own oxygen mask) that the answer is 'none'.

It's instinctual that we look after someone else's needs before our own. Biologically, we're programmed to protect our children and the young. But we're no longer being hunted by woolly mammoths. And, for the majority of us, our professional and personal lives are not a matter of life and death.

Through time, through society, through cultural norms, hell even through advertising, we've been taught to continue putting others' needs before our own. That doing anything else is selfish! That we must push on — no complaints, no time to take a break! Stopping is for losers. You don't get to the top by sitting down the bottom, right? Not when Penny manages to run the division, bring in the big bucks, make packed lunches for the kids, take them swimming *and* bake cookies for her team on a Thursday night.

The result? We bury our own needs; we keep pushing. We forget about putting our oxygen mask on first. In fact, we may as well throw it out the window.

The thing is that putting your own needs first is not being selfish; it is being smart.

Think about it for a minute. If you don't have your own oxygen mask on, then you might pass out before you can fit someone else's!

So, if you're always *doing*, if you're ticking off all the things on your to-do list, never taking a break, attending to the demands and pressures of everyone else, then what do you think is going to happen?

You're going to burn out, that's what.

I think we're being unconsciously told to push past our limits — to not listen to our inner voices telling us to stop and relax, but instead listening to the external voices telling us to keep on going ...

Burnout is real. Emotional and physical exhaustion is real. Brain fog is real. And the warning signs are there, but it's too easy not to notice them. We keep going to work, totting up those hours, pumping our bodies in the gym, living on strange diets and then we wonder why we finally crash.

Sucking it up will result in you f*cking it up.

Plain and simple!

How many of you would admit to regularly feeling like a champagne bottle that's been shaken so much the cork feels like it will pop at any moment?

Too often it's because we're self-sabotaging by giving too much to others and not enough to ourselves. This means you're doing a disservice to everyone else around you because you're pushing yourself to the limit. I mean, how can you be good to anyone else if you're not being good to yourself?

This is not being selfish; this is called self-care.

It's about managing your personal stamina for your success as well as others'.

So how would you rate yourself in terms of how you're showing up right now for yourself and your team, for your clients and your family?

If your stamina were a pendulum swinging from left to right — from surviving to being on fire and thriving — where would that pendulum stop?

Stop telling yourself fake stories

I used to think I had all the answers. That no-one in my team could do it like me. If someone didn't deliver, then I'd just take over and do it myself. It somehow felt wrong to ask for help — like if I did that, it would be admitting failure. Here are some of my favourite stories I would tell myself that would justify why I was feeling stretched, tired and overwhelmed and why my stamina was taking a beating.

Which ones ring true for you?

Story 1: everyone in my industry works like this

Really? Or are you all just copying one another's madness?

Jeffrey Pfeffer, in his book *Dying for a Paycheck,* points out,

> *In a perverse twist, longer work hours have become a status symbol — a marker of how important, indeed indispensable, someone is... As such, people want to put in long hours to signal how valuable they are.*

In the past, when I looked at the ridiculous hours I saw others putting in, I thought I had to work these hours too, to get noticed, to be doing the 'right thing', to be successful. I'd work into the night, at weekends, checking my phone at all times of the day — even when I was supposed to be relaxing on holiday. I mean, only wimps need time off, right? What I failed to recognise and learn from was the other people in the industry who were succeeding *without putting in these crazy hours*. My frame of reference was totally warped. Maybe yours is too?

Story 2: I've worked out how to survive on 6 hours' sleep

Really? And how's that working out for you?

When I used to wear this badge, I had no idea that the lack of sleep was challenging my patience and ability to remain calm under pressure, and as for being a present leader, partner and parent—what's that? As Arianna Huffington shares in her book *Thrive*, sleep is the fifth pillar of success as it creates better cognition, less stress and higher life satisfaction. A RAND Corporation study actually states, 'A person who sleeps on average less than six hours a night has a 13 per cent higher mortality risk than someone sleeping between seven and nine hours'. Wow.

Need more convincing? A 2000 study by AM Williamson and Anne-Marie Feyer shows that moderate sleep deprivation produces impairments equivalent to those of alcohol intoxication. Yikes!

Story 3: I can multitask

Really? How many balls did you drop last week?

Women are supposed to be awesome at this, right? I'd juggle the balls of work and home, boss and friend, parent and partner, project plans and grocery lists. I thought I was a genius at creating lists within lists, but in reality, deadlines were missed, details forgotten, school lunches left in fridges, appointments missed. I was definitely doing a lot of stuff—but not necessarily doing a lot of stuff well.

Take note of David Meyer, a professor of psychology at the University of Michigan and director of the school's Brain, Cognition and Action Laboratory, who said,

> *Once you start to make things more complicated, things get messier, and as a result, there's going to be interference with one or more of the tasks. Either you're going to have to slow down on one of the tasks, or you're going to start making mistakes.*

Story 4: I don't have time to look after myself

Really? What is the opportunity cost?

Limited exercise or excessive exercise to the point of exhaustion, poor diet, lack of sleep, a few too many drinks … I can still remember being on a retreat in the early days of my own business when the children were still little and having a coffee conversation with wellness expert Nikki Fogden-Moore. She said something that touched a nerve and produced a flood of tears: 'Janine, we can't FedEx our bodies back'. Aka, we buy back time by looking after ourselves, people!

Story 5: Being a perfect parent means doing everything

Really? According to whom?

Everyone knows them: the perfect parent. Yet in reality *they don't exist!* Parent guilt and the illusion of a work–life balance — that's right because it's an *illusion.* I felt incredibly isolated because society told me it wasn't right to pursue a career while apparently missing the critical early years of my children. Talk about being eaten up from the inside out. I felt like I was existing and going through the motions. I reckon I failed a few times at a number of things, very likely reacted inappropriately in some situations, lost friends in the process because instead of asking for help I backed away and spent a long time hiding behind the armour of 'fake it till you make it'.

For me, there was no one moment of realisation — but more a series of moments where the penny finally dropped …

Too many of us think that to be successful we have to work ourselves to the bone, but this needs to stop!

Becoming your brilliant self is all about being strategic with your energy and your resources. It's about taking care of yourself first and foremost.

So what stories are you telling yourself that are working against you instead of for you?

Get up now and turn your own fake-news channel off!

How many plates?

In the book, *The Power of Full Engagement*, Dr Jim Loehr and Tony Schwartz suggest that the main reason why some people achieve 10 times more in any given day than most people do in weeks, is not because they manage time better — it's because they've learned how to manage and balance their energy across physical, emotional, mental and spiritual components.

This concept of managing and balancing energy across various facets of our lives was discussed in a 2009 *New Yorker* article, where author David Sedaris shared the Four Burners Theory. He'd heard this theory while driving with his unofficial tour guide, a woman named Pat, during a trip to Australia, and she'd heard about the theory at a management seminar she'd attended. The theory goes that like a gas stove we all have four burners: family, friends, health and work. In order to be successful, you have to switch off one of your burners. In order to be *really* successful, you have to cut off two.

The theory here is that we can't have it all. We have to make a choice as to what we're going to give up in order to gain.

Now I actually do believe we can have it all, but just not at the same time and not *all* of the time. It's not about giving anything up but more about where you decide to invest your energy at a given point in time.

Sometimes we have to make a choice to invest more time into some areas of our lives and less into others so that everything doesn't come crashing down around us all at once.

Have you ever seen a street juggler spinning multiple plates on the end of sticks, masterfully ensuring the right speed and energy to prevent any plates from crashing to the ground? Let's imagine for a moment that you're that juggler with one stick in each hand and one stick somehow being held between your toes. On the end of each stick is a plate and your job is to keep each plate spinning and, in the air, doing whatever you need to do to ensure no plate crashes to the ground. Each plate represents one specific area of your life:

1. Plate #1 represents your work and career and how well you feel you're doing.

2. Plate #2 represents the most important people and relationships in your world — the people who feed your soul — and how you're doing in terms of managing the relationships.

3. Plate #3 represents you: your stamina, happiness and general wellbeing and how you're really doing.

If you had to mark yourself out of five in terms of how successfully you're spinning each plate and how satisfied you are, right now, with 5 being awesome and 0 being a risk of crashing, how would you rate?

Now think about what you need to do to help each plate spin better, to improve your score, to prevent the plate from crashing.

◆   What do you need to *stop* doing?

◆   What do you need to *start* doing?

Not all plates have to spin equally at the same height, but they all need some level of intentional investment to stop crashing.

If the relationship plate is close to crashing, what do you need to do to lift it? If the career business plate is starting to lose momentum, what do you need to do to refuel it? What about you: what do you need to do, just for you, to ensure you're harnessing your energy in the best way possible? And which plate right now is okay to be spinning that little bit lower than the others?

Sometimes work needs more energy and time; sometimes you have to slow down on the work because the important relationships of partners, family and children need attention. And sometimes you need to attach the oxygen mask to yourself, to take a break. Recharge the batteries. Oxygenate your brain! It may be for half an hour — it may be for a week. But don't feel guilty for putting yourself first. Because in the end a little TLC will benefit everyone in your life, professionally and personally.

I don't believe we have to completely cut off key areas of our lives. It doesn't have to be the ultimatum of 'either this or that'. While life is full of trade-offs — I absolutely believe it can be a 'this and that' — we have to be cognisant of ourselves, take ownership of the choices we make and be intentional about deciding where we're investing our energy and our time: what we're doing, when and with whom to ensure that all our plates keep spinning above the ground and our personal stamina is maintained.

Harnessing your energy means keeping all the plates spinning, so one or more don't crash on the floor and become irreplaceable.

The opportunity cost of 'no'

How many times have you said 'yes' to something, when deep down you know you should say 'no'?

Whether it be saying 'no' to an appointment that isn't going to add value to either party, to taking on a piece of work that you haven't got time to deliver or to a simple to-do when your day is already jam packed, these two simple letters when put together seem to cripple the best of us.

Every 'yes' we commit to invariably means we're saying 'no' to something else.

Like in economics, there's a trade-off every time. Every 'yes' has an investment in time, money or energy (often all three), and this investment means you don't have the time, money or energy to invest in something else. Like yin and yang, black and white, night and day, 'yes' and 'no' are inextricably linked.

In his blog, 'Opportunity costs just went up', Seth Godin states that 'opportunity cost is the key to making decisions'. He adds that knowing the value of what you're giving up makes you wiser in your choices. Once you know the value of the alternatives you're giving up, you can be smarter about what you're choosing to do. Time is not infinite and any given hour only comes up once before it's gone forever. This means that choosing how to spend or invest our time comes with opportunity costs.

During my training and mentoring I talk a lot about the opportunity cost of decision making and how we seem to focus on the gain of every opportunity that comes our way — for example, I need to take that piece of work because it could add people to my database, or it may lead to some media coverage, or another sale somewhere down the track. But what about the loss?

The cost of that yes is always time, energy, focus and sometimes money away from the very thing that actually needs your attention most.

And why? Why do we find it so hard to say 'no'? Is it our innate desire to please? A need to feel wanted? Or simply because we don't want to hurt someone else's feelings?

'"No" may be the most powerful word in the language, but it's also potentially the most destructive, which is why it's hard to say,' says William Ury, director of the Global Negotiation Project at Harvard University. Ury explains that 'no' is hard to say because it creates 'tension between exercising your power and tending to your relationship'.

Whatever the reason, saying 'yes' can create stress, tension and ultimately compromise quality. Those 'yeses' challenge the ability to think clearly and rationally. They can impact the delivery of major goals and milestones. It may actually mean we move towards our vision in first gear instead of fifth because we've taken a detour off track, around the back of all the trees. (Know that saying, 'Can't see the wood for the trees'? ...)

I can still remember sitting down with my mentor, Matt Church, a few years ago debating the various options available to me in terms of where to take my business next. I was sharing other people's opinions, what existing clients wanted and bigger picture plans A, B and C — all of which looked mightily attractive. He looked at me calmly and said, 'Janine, just because you can doesn't mean you should'.

What he was advising me to do was align my 'yeses' to my bigger picture vision and to be courageous enough to say 'no' to some good-lookin' opportunities that weren't going to get me closer to my end goal.

As American author Darren Hardy explains in a *Success* magazine article titled 'Success is not about what you DO...', 'When it comes to comparing superachievers and everyone else, it has less to do with what they do and more to do with what they *don't* do'.

Hardy is right. Successful people know how to put a big fat strike through the non-essentials: they deflect low-priority work and decisions; run streamlined meetings; remove meetings from their calendars; and allocate time for reflection, high-quality thinking and their own health and wellbeing. They are intentional about how they manage their time and consequently their energy.

One of the tools I suggest to my clients to help them navigate decision making is to develop a personal Decision-Making Triage.

Here's how it works.

Thinking about your overarching objective — for example, should my business sponsor a stand at an industry conference — what are the three critical elements and questions you'd need to answer 'yes' to for it to go ahead? (See figure 5.1.)

For example, the three elements could be:

1. *sales*: Does this decision lead to sales generation? (Y/N)

2. *time*: Does this decision support time on the bigger vision we're chasing? (Y/N)

3. *desire*: Does this decision involve working with people I want to work with? (Y/N)

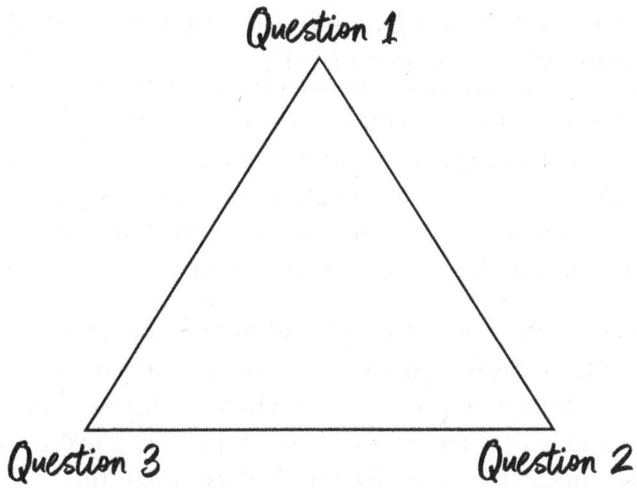

Figure 5.1: the decision-making triage

When a decision needs to be made, the opportunity exists to pause and to review the decision against the triage, and only if you can answer 'yes' to each of the three elements is it a 'yes'. Two or one out of three is not a good enough reason.

How could you implement the decision-making triage in your life?

What is one big goal you're working towards?

What are the three questions you could ask yourself to help you stay on track?

Say 'no' when things don't align to your values, priorities and goals. Say 'yes' to the projects that matter to you, your career and your life.

Help!

A few years ago, I competed in a Tough Mudder. At the time it was marketed as 'one of the hardest obstacle courses in the world', a 20-kilometre course of mud with challenging obstacles created by British Special Forces soldiers. (Did I mention the mud?)

About 16 kilometres into the course, already exhausted, covered in cuts and bruises, body feeling battered and caked in muck, I reached the next obstacle — Everest. Looming ahead of me was a quarter pipe standing at over 4.5 metres tall, with a curved top just to make it that little bit harder to grab... and our challenge? To get to the top of it.

I saw people running at it full pelt and not getting anywhere; bodies slamming into the wall and sliding unceremoniously to the ground; arms and legs being stretched as people hung on for dear life and body parts were grabbed as teammates tried to pull each other up. People looked exhausted. It looked really hard and really painful.

What did I do?

I panicked! My inner voice went into 'I can't, I can't' overdrive and there's no doubt my amygdala was having its own party of 'you're going to hurt yourself; you're going to fail', playing on repeat and at full blast. The tears started to roll and I froze.

After much cajoling and voices of encouragement, some very deep breaths from me and a shout of, 'C'mon Janine, Put Your Big Girl Pants On', I pulled myself together and got my brain to connect to my legs to run. I tried once, twice, three times and finally made it thanks to the support of my teammates.

The workplace is a lot like the Tough Mudder field, with people elbowing each other, competing for first place (but maybe without the mud). We may be swamped with work, have a major challenge we're trying to complete, a tricky client we're having to placate, a significant business pitch we're leading, a challenging relationship at work, or we may well have truly f*cked something up and don't know what to do next. Yet instead of looking to our colleagues to ask for help we try and go it alone.

And why?

We think that asking for help is a sign of weakness and incompetence.

We want to show that we're self-reliant. We think it's going to show others our vulnerabilities and therefore affect our future and our career prospects. But asking for help can actually be the difference between success and failure. We can't be successful alone. We need others to help strengthen us, to feed our stamina, to encourage us to keep going. Asking for help shows humility and strength.

The reality is we all have bad days, days when things don't go right, where that deal falls over, the client becomes challenging, the staff member storms out of the meeting. It's okay to sit in a bad day for a short time — to use it as a moment to reset, to call your bestie and have a moan, rant, cry or beer — but it's your ability to pull yourself out and to recover that counts. This is where we often need to reach out and ask for help to reset and restart. To remember that tomorrow is another day.

Dr Paul Schempp, an award-winning research professor at the University of Georgia known as 'The Expert on Expertise', has led several studies that have consistently shown a willingness to ask for help as one of the largest differentiators between extraordinary achievers and ordinary achievers. 'Leaders who ask for and accept input from team members are more successful and inspirational than leaders who believe they need to go it alone,' says Schempp.

So next time you don't know what to do or which way to turn, when you feel your stamina needs a reboot, don't give up. Instead reach out to your support network and ask for help.

Successful people know who they can rely on and they ask for help.

Brilliance in action

1. Find fake

Identify the stories you may be telling yourself to justify how you're living and leading. Are these true? Or are they actually negatively impacting your ability to influence and be your brilliant self?

2. Spin plates

Think about the plates you're currently spinning.

1. Plate #1 represents your work and career and how well you feel you're doing.

2. Plate #2 represents the most important people and relationships in your world, the people who feed your soul.

3. Plate #3 represents you: your stamina, happiness and general wellbeing and how you're really doing.

Mark how you're doing for each plate in terms of satisfaction level, with 5 being awesome and 0 being terrible.

1. Plate 1 (work and career) = ... out of 5

2. Plate 2 (relationship) = ... out of 5

3. Plate 3 (me) = ... out of 5

    ◆ What do you notice?

    ◆ Are you happy with the self-assessment?

    ◆ Are there areas you want to improve?

    ◆ Which plate isn't getting any love?

- ◆ What are the one or two things you could do to get your plates spinning more in alignment with what you'd like?

- ◆ What help do you need?

Keep coming back to this self-assessment throughout the year and at key times. It's amazing how simple, yet effective, it is for recognising when and where you need to slow down or speed up.

3. Decide on your triage

Take the time to consider your three critical questions for your decision-making triage. This will help you say 'yes' to the things that really matter and 'no' to the things that could potentially distract you or take you off course.

Facet 6

Behaviour

My niece Emily started swimming 200-metre backstroke competitively when she was 10 years old. She recalls one race, when she was 12, when she was standing in the marshalling room and feeling so nervous that she started crying. It was only her mum shouting, 'You can do it, Em' that made her jump in the pool, push through and achieve a personal best race time of 3:03:78 and with this a qualification for the Adelaide State Championship. Her subsequent feeling of euphoria ignited a passion to keep swimming.

Two years later, Emily was swimming 2:24.60 and was ranked seventh in the state of Victoria, Australia, with a goal of achieving a national time to compete at a higher level again. While her big-picture vision is well and truly planted in her psyche, it is her commitment to daily actions and behaviours that ensures her incremental improvements. She trains 11 times a week, three of those in the gym and eight in the pool, and has to sacrifice a lot along the way. As Emily shares, 'Usually I get friends asking to catch up or go out on the weekend or to a party but most of the time I have a swim meet and as hard as it is to say no I have to because I know that I have a goal to reach and to reach that goal I have to train'.

Success isn't something you simply stumble upon. It's a reward for having ceaseless tenacity and a consistent and repetitive commitment to the right behaviours.

According to self-development speaker Brian Tracy (who has authored over 70 books!) habits determine 95 per cent of a person's behaviour. When I think about establishing and committing to good behaviours and habits to achieve a goal, I think about Emily and her 11 training sessions a week.

Imagine what you could achieve if, just like Emily, you implemented the equivalent of your own training program? With the right habits and behaviours, how could you continually improve your personal best and keep the fire of your brilliance burning?

Everything we dream of achieving *is possible*, but it needs you to do the work and adopt the right behaviours.

Becoming a master of self-discipline is the number one trait needed to accomplish any goal or anything in life. Deciding what behaviours you will adopt versus what you won't is the tipping point between moving towards success and stalling along the way.

> **Saying 'I can' or even 'This year my goal is to …' is one thing; undertaking the right actions and behaviours to bring that to life is the game changer.**

A game of inches

Charles Duhigg, author of *The Power of Habit* and an expert on behavioural psychology, suggests that most people fail to adopt new behaviours because they don't understand the structure of habits. Duhigg refers to the habit loop — a three-part process (cue, routine and reward) — within our brain that controls how habits are formed, and if any of these three parts are missed the habit is broken.

He says that first a *cue* 'tells your brain to go into automatic mode and which habit to use'. Next, he maintains, is a 'physical, mental or emotional' *routine*. And lastly is the *reward*, which, he says, 'helps your brain figure out if this habit loop is worth remembering for the future'.

Your behaviours, your habits, your actions — whatever you choose to call them — matter if you're going to be brilliant.

Now, this is not a book just about high-performance habits. There are some incredible thought leaders in this space that I recommend you check out. My favourites are James Clear (*Atomic Habits*), Brendon Burchard (*The Motivation Manifesto*) and Jeff Olson (*The Slight Edge*).

What I love about the thinking around habits in these books is the concept of daily habits. That if we break down our big goals into small, daily habitual actions, ultimately over time we will achieve the big-picture aim.

It's only through continuous and consistent behaviours that the compound effect of the activity will kick in and create traction.

In the movie, *Any Given Sunday*, Al Pacino's character, Tony D'Amato, describes improvements as inches:

> *You find out that life is just a game of inches. So is football. Because in either game, life or football, the margin for error is so small ... when we add up all those inches that's going to make the fucking difference between winning and losing.*

Jeff Olson reinforces this in *The Slight Edge*:

> *You already know how to do everything ... to make you an outrageous success. All you have to do is keep doing the things that have gotten you this far ...*

> *Simple daily disciplines — little productive actions, repeated consistently over time — add up to the difference between failure and success.*

Olson even goes as far as codifying his thinking into a formula: 'Consistently repeated daily actions + time = inconquerable results.'

There's one common thread that connects Olson, Clear, Burchard, and even Pacino's character in the movie: you can't sit around waiting for success to happen, you have to make it come to you through the actions you take. It's up to you to take control because everything you do matters. You can either choose to fuel your habit tank or deplete it. There's no instant win, but rather the accumulation of daily habits over time that deliver massive results.

So, what are your daily habits? Calling five potential clients a day, posting one blog a week, reading 20 pages of a book every day, exercising for 30 minutes, or just 10 minutes to sit and think? The critical thing is to own the habits that you know will fuel the right action *for you.*

Where are you now (Point A) and where do you want to go (Point B)? The gap between these two end points is where the right action and right habits have to live. What do you need to do consistently to fuel your habit tank to move from A and get closer to B?

In *Atomic Habits*, James Clear shares four key laws for creating good habits:

1. Make it obvious

2. Make it attractive

3. Make it easy

4. Make it satisfying.

When it comes to adopting the right behaviours to fuel the habit tank, I work on five key principles. Try them and see.

1. *Set your intention*: Identify what you want to achieve and get clear on the actions, on the small steps, you need to take to get there.

2. *Stop wishing and start doing*: Act! Just setting goals doesn't define achievement. It's the actions we take every day that contribute to achieving the goals, habits and behaviours we put in place.

3. *Pay attention to your goals*: Check progress. Focusing on the right work at the right time and managing distractions along the way is a priority. Every day or week I check in on my progress and ask myself, How did I do? What needs to be tweaked?

4. *Commit to getting back up*: Stop and acknowledge when things go wrong; identify why and what the learning lesson is before starting again. Resetting is the key. Giving up is not an option. It's okay to be flawsome! It's okay that some days things don't go to plan — that's life, right? Don't beat yourself up, but don't give up either.

5. *Surround yourself with the right people*: Embrace those who are going to support your habits and move away from the time wasters (we'll discuss this more in Law 3).

Commit to adopting the right behaviours and success will come to you.

Go for green

Psychologist and author Dr Rick Hanson described the brain as having three states: red, orange and green.

The red brain is often described as a state of stress. In this stage, the hormones cortisol and adrenaline are released, creating effects such as tunnel vision, muscle tension, judgemental thinking, a narrow point of view and increased stress levels. The same physical and psychological effects happen if we don't adopt actions and behaviours to support a positive growth mindset and the maintenance of our stamina. If we don't get enough sleep, when we run ourselves ragged, if we have no time to stop, to think, to reset, to re-energise we risk running ourselves mentally, physically and emotionally into the ground. The result is we lose perspective, we enter overwhelm and actions become reactive as we feel out of control and is if we're swimming against the tide. We enter the red zone.

The orange brain is described as the neutral, middle ground or going through the motions of getting stuff done.

What we need to aspire to is the equivalent of the green brain and a state of calmness and feeling in control and in flow. In this state, cortisol and adrenaline are reduced and the 'happy' hormone, oxytocin, comes out to play, resulting in increased perspective, self-awareness, empathy for others and a more relaxed state of being.

The daily behaviours that you adopt (or not) will put you in the red, orange or green brain states. So which behaviours are you choosing?

When we consistently adopt the right actions and behaviours that fuel our mindset and stamina in a good way, we feel present and connected, a wider perspective feeds creativity and curiosity, and we're able to think clearly, innovate, ideate and make calm and well-thought-through decisions. We're in the green brain state.

Think about where you'd put yourself right now as you're reading this book.

Do you feel like you're in the green brain state, in control of your personal boundaries and non-negotiables: you know what you are doing and when and understand your everyday behaviours are necessary to fuelling your brilliance?

Or, are you feeling more in the red brain state: out of control and in overwhelm as your good behaviour intentions slip down the priority ladder—maybe you've become a slave to others and their priorities, instead?

Leader Ray Pittman, first mentioned in Law 1, shared with me that he used to have a 'failed diary'. His continuous 'yes' resulted in numerous plates spinning across endless back-to-back meetings and phone calls discussing numerous projects because he felt, in his own words, that he 'had to be all things to all people to be the leader'. His 'failed diary' meant there was no blank space to think, to gain perspective on the next key decision for the business or even gaps to enjoy rejuvenating 'me' time. He admits that on reflection 'overloading my diary was a failed strategy for me' as he let the habits and behaviours that he knew fuelled his success fall by the wayside. Ray had entered the red zone.

There's nothing heroic about becoming a slave to your diary and other people's requirements. This is not aligned to maintaining the behaviours needed to be ready, to be brilliant. In fact, it's the fast-track to burnout and a whole heap of challenging mindset issues. We risk overwhelm, falling into the 'I'm so busy' trap. We find it hard to navigate the murkiness to find the clarity; we go into work avoidance, making excuses and shaking any accountability off ourselves, instead blaming others for our lack of progress. And as for those projects that matter and brilliant behaviours you know you need to re-implement to get things back on track? Well, they get thrown out with the trash!

Unleashing brilliance requires you to be highly disciplined; to adopt the right behaviours to fuel your mindset and stamina in the right direction in order to keep you in the green brain state of momentum and progress.

Being 'in the green' at all times is an unrealistic expectation. It's how you get yourself back on track that counts.

Ray realised that his 'failed diary' was not conducive to his performance or leadership. He knew he had to reclaim his green brain state to fuel his brilliant performance. He knew that the key behaviours to support his stamina and mindset were around being disciplined with time, conserving his energy and mental capacity for the right work where he could truly add value, and ensuring that he built into his calendar the 'me' time he needed to do the things that refuelled his energy. So he took charge and actively created blank space to think, to create, to strategise, to think about the business and next steps. He reset boundaries and intentions and realigned his behaviours to his key goals. He shared, 'Success for me now looks like a clear diary with chunks of time for refreshing and sharpening the saw and the time to make important decisions'.

Nicole Eckels, co-founder of Sapphire Group and CEO of Glasshouse Fragrances, provided the same insight during her time on my podcast. She said, 'I don't fill up my time with social engagements. I used to, but then I had no time to reflect. I do my best thinking when I'm getting ready or when I'm on a walk or pottering around. This is now sacred time for me that I carve off because it's important for my performance'.

We can't expand time (as much as we'd love to). It's up to you to make time matter. Get clear on the behaviours that bring out your brilliant self and keep you in the green brain state for as long as possible. Think about what behaviours support your bigger plan. These could relate to the three areas of:

1. What do you need to read, listen to or think about to fuel you mentally?

2. What do you need to do to fuel yourself spiritually and physically?

3. Who do you need to hang with to feed yourself positivity and inspiration and fuel you emotionally?

> **You have to test, review, reset and test again to determine the right behaviours to support continued uphill momentum.**

Progress delusion

In his book *How to Lead a Quest*, Dr Jason Fox shares the concept of 'progress delusion'. He describes this as 'the state where we find ourselves saying yes to so many little things that the biggest, more important things suffer'.

Sound familiar?

The definition of progress is the forward or onward momentum in the direction of your goals and dreams. But how much progress are you really making each day? Or are you simply ticking off meaningless tasks on a to-do list to *feel* like you're making progress?

> **Are you lost in a flurry of unimportant actions, 'Yay-I-cleared-my-inbox' moments, high-fives and short-lived happy dances?**

While we know sitting on Facebook for 30 minutes giggling at cat videos, putting things on a list that you've already done just so you can tick them off, watching three episodes consecutively of *Billions*, or colour-coding the books on your bookshelf (is that just me?) will have detrimental effects on our momentum, we equally love that addictive, short-term fix of dopamine to the brain!

According to AsapSCIENCE's video on procrastination,

> *Every time something enjoyable happens, you get a dose of dopamine, which modifies the neurons in your brain, making you more likely to repeat this behaviour... Often times procrastination is a symptom, not a cause.*

It's easy to give in to progress delusion and receiving that instant endorphin rush of the high and the pleasure it brings. But this joy is definitely short-lived. It's so much harder to choose the delayed gratification of the discipline needed to take the right actions because, let's be honest, it can be a little bit boring, even though we know the long-term benefit will pay off.

Big goals are things like building a profitable business — this is always the culmination of a series of decisions and actions; or achieving a big promotion as the result of the work you've done, the results achieved and the skills you have. None of this happens overnight. And while we know this to be true, many of us whittle away the time on never-ending 'to-do' lists to make us feel good about putting a big fat tick next to things like 'eat lunch'.

In his book *The Motivation Manifesto*, Brendon Burchard says that the first spark of motivation happens when an ambition (dream, big goal) is aligned with an expectancy (belief) that you can achieve your ambition. He argues that this is just the beginning and that only by constantly paying attention to (focusing on) your ambition and expectancy can you sustain motivation over time. Without attention, he argues, the risk is we lose focus, we get taken off track, we adopt the wrong action and face the distraction of following shiny stuff. This is where most people fail!

To add to this, we need to pay attention to our positive behaviours, which support our mindset and stamina and help us harness energy over time.

Mindset + Stamina + Positive Key Behaviours = Harnessed Energy Over Time

High performers pay attention to their positive behaviours and adopt an excuse-free life. They master the art of maintaining sustained energy and the effort required, and they take ownership of their actions — and this drives excellence over time.

Ultimately, you've got to be patient; you've got to be consistent.

Don't add little tasks here and there to the noise — that's essentially a distraction!

What are the key milestones you need to achieve along the way?

Chase progress over perfection

I have two friends, Alison and Sarah, who are both marathon runners. In 2018 they trained hard, individually, to run the New York City Marathon.

Alison is a corporate executive and fitness fanatic, spending most weekends cycling or running — she tells me it's her happy place. Alison's already clocked up five bike rides across Thailand totalling 3300 kilometres, raising money for the charity Hands Across the Water. She is an inspiration.

Sarah, on the other hand, is a business owner, mother of three primary-school-aged children and admitted that she 'hadn't run, except after an errant child, in around 15 years'. Yet, she's equally an inspiration, and here's why.

Both Alison and Sarah trained hard for the event, every week pounding the streets, upping their times, battling injury and fighting mindset struggles, all in a bid to hit the magic moment, the finish line at the marathon.

On the day of the race, Alison ended up running with a knee injury that got more and more painful the more she ran. Yet she was determined to finish, even when she stopped at the first aid tent, threw up, got treatment and went on to finish in five hours and eight minutes. Alison was glad she finished but was really vocal about her disappointment at not getting under her target of four hours.

Sarah made it across the finish line in tears, after dark, with barely anyone around in about 7.5 hours. What's even more incredible is that during the last couple of kilometres, Sarah came across a fellow runner, a doctor who was on her sixth marathon. This runner was dehydrated, staggering along the course and barely able to talk. So Sarah helped her across the finish line, too! She was on cloud 9!

What's interesting here are the stories both Alison and Sarah told themselves.

Same race. Different end times. Different stories around success.

In my mind, both succeeded as each battled their inner demons and won. Each got over the finish line and each learned something about themselves to take into the next race.

Yet it's too easy to beat ourselves up when our story doesn't play out in real life as it does in our head.

Alison was disappointed that she didn't get under her four-hour target, which would have been a breakthrough achievement, even though she battled an injury, and nearly fainted!

We spend a lot of time and energy seeking big breakthroughs, moments that are incredibly satisfying, yet extremely hard to come by. They're called breakthroughs because they're rare.

Focusing only on the breakthroughs can lead to constant disappointment and frustration. A focus on the big-picture goal can cause you to lose sight of the smaller, incremental improvements that will form the building blocks of your success.

You've got to celebrate progress over perfection because the payoffs of a 'small win' are equally important.

In the article, 'Pieces of the leadership puzzle' for the Institute of Managers and Leaders, Daniel Flynn, co-founder of Thankyou—the social enterprise that directs its profits from sales of water, food, body care and baby products towards ending global poverty—states that celebrating the small wins as well as the big ones is critical.

In the article, he shares the story of being challenged by his mentor on how he celebrates the small wins. Flynn recalls, 'I had nothing. I am so driven by the future and where we need to go, the next opportunity, the impact we can make, the markets we could and should be in.'

Flynn recognised that by not celebrating the small wins—the progress being made—but rather always focusing on the big end goal and breakthrough, he was creating the same push and drive among his team. While this may seem okay, the reality, he recognised, was that he was risking team burnout.

Flynn shares, 'I'm still not perfect at it but I'm trying to get better', and on a weekly basis Thankyou now celebrates small things teams and individuals have done.

Celebrate the small stuff. Seeking and acknowledging small improvements one day at a time fuels the feeling of forward momentum and achievement.

Give yourself something to look forward to:

◆ a walk on the beach

◆ dinner with friends

- ◆ an early pass at work

- ◆ reading a good book

- ◆ a bottle of your favourite wine

- ◆ snuggling on the sofa and watching a movie.

What could you celebrate this week and how will you celebrate it?

Channel your inner Dory

There's a special place in my heart for the movie *Finding Nemo*. This was 'The One'. The one movie I could play on repeat to my kids and they could recite the script nearly word-for-word. My favourite line is when Dory sings to Nemo:

When life gets you down, you know what 'chu gotta do?

Just keep swimming.

Just keep swimming.

Just keep swimming, swimming, swimming.

The same can be said for our behaviours! When we fall off the good-behaviour train and land on our faces in a whole heap of, 'I've done it again', we have to acknowledge, learn and get back up, reset and get back at it—or in the wise words of Dory, 'Just keep swimming'.

In my *Unleashing Brilliance* podcast with Jack Delosa, founder of The Entourage and listed in the *BRW* Young Rich List since 2014, we discussed the benefit of daily habits and tracking performance. Jack agreed that, like many of us, it's hard to achieve 100 per cent every day and that on those not-so-great days, you stumble, acknowledge what happened and move on. He said, 'Don't beat yourself up and then use this as an excuse to give up—accept, note the learning and move forward'.

Pay attention to your goal, track your progress and try for that 1 per cent.

Brilliance in action

1. Daily habit tracker

Identify up to five daily habits that you know drive better performance for you. Is it five sales calls, 10 minutes' meditation, taking a lunch break?

Use a pen and paper checklist by writing them down and every day track how you do. Alternatively, go digital and download an online habit tracking tool. Some suggestions include Streaks, Habitshare, Tally and Strides.

2. Go for green

Are you operating in the red brain state or the green brain state? What do you need to change to maximise your time in the green brain state?

3. Reward yourself

What's the one key thing you want to do differently this month and why does it matter? What's your reward for doing this one month from now? And, just to be serious, what's your consequence if you don't do this one month from now?

Great! Now find an accountability buddy. Commit, share and action!

Watch out!

No matter our best intentions, Law 2 and harnessing your energy appears to be one of the hardest things to practise given the increasing levels of burnout, exhaustion and poor mental health we're seeing across the world.

Ultimately, each of us has to take ownership and control of our own stamina and vitality. But there are three shadows that we need to watch out for. These negate energy, dampen passion and put a brake on momentum.

These antitheses of Law 2 are:

1. Blame-itis

2. Distraction

3. Burnout.

Let's explore each now so you know what you have to watch out for.

1. Blame-itis

'It wasn't me—it was him/her ...'

'I tried but they wouldn't let me ...'

'It's too hard to do that ...'

'I didn't make it because (insert relevant excuse) got in the way.'

'Sorry I missed that email; it must have got lost in the internet ether.'

The myriad excuses for why we didn't achieve, while others did, can be heard loud and clear right across workplaces and in our personal lives. It's incredible how many people these days blame others and work through an endless excuse list they hope will keep them off the hook. Every time we make an excuse and blame someone or something else external to us, we deflect from ourselves, which ultimately means we're not learning a lesson or taking ownership for our own actions.

We've all heard them (and maybe even said them ourselves): 'Well, they've got the contacts / the client base / the thousands of followers / the budgets / the team / the experience / the resources and they don't have [insert whatever you have that you feel is getting in the way].'

Blame-itis is, quite simply, not accepting responsibility for any of your actions or accountability for your own behaviours.

It's about making excuses and not accepting that maybe, just maybe, you did play a critical part in things not quite going to plan. That, actually, it isn't anyone else's fault that you didn't achieve your goals over the past 12 months—it's yours.

So how do you cure a case of blame-itis?

Of course, we all have different baggage, backgrounds, financial situations and stuff going on. But if you want it enough, if you're hungry enough and if you take control of owning your role in writing your story, creating your own dreams, then action happens.

Whether things go to plan or not, hold yourself 100 per cent accountable for the outcome, whatever it may be. Dwelling on the small stuff can be debilitating. We end up in a never-ending cycle of 'coulda, shoulda, woulda'. Unless we let go of the blame game and finger pointing, accept what happened and embrace the learnings from the situation, we're unable to move forward.

The choice is yours: sit in a quagmire of excuses and the resulting sludge of status quo or accept that things didn't quite go to plan, re-group, re-plan and move on.

It's not about making excuses or quitting the game. It's simply about considering that perhaps you may somehow have contributed to the end result.

Own the role you have to play and hold yourself accountable for your own successes and failures, whatever they may be, because this will absolutely create action towards achieving your goals.

Who or what are you blaming for a lack of your own inaction? How can you stop this?

What excuses have become part of your life? How can you flip these on their head and create the counter argument?

2. Distraction

These are the small distractions that appear at every opportune moment as a little voice in your head, directly in your line of sight or even at the hands of others with exactly the thing you love and desire. It could be a chocolate bar, another 'not so' quick check of Facebook, yet another excuse to leave your work station because the coffee machine is calling or it could be another night out with friends vs. staying home, going to the gym, finishing that proposal, reading that paper (insert relevant task).

And there are the bigger distractions that act as massive deviations off the road: the new sale that may not actually be your ideal client, may be misaligned with your business focus or may even be a contract that looks great on paper but deviates from something else you're trying to win.

And more often than not distraction wins—especially if there's some guilt attached to it! Guilt for not saying 'yes' to that very persuasive client. Guilt for not making sure your lounge looks like the cover of *Houses* magazine, or for not baking a cake for the kids' school fair.

It doesn't matter what the challenge is for you—a personal fitness challenge, pulling together a business proposal, working on your business growth plans, hustling for sales or doing whatever it takes to secure the next promotion—the daily battle is very real.

It's easy to give in to distraction, receiving that instant endorphin rush of the high and the pleasure it brings. But this joy is definitely short-lived. When you fall to distraction, the key is not to beat yourself up. Forgive yourself. Keep moving forward.

What are the biggest distractions for you?

What do you need to do to minimise these distractions to help you stay focused?

3. Burnout

Debbie O'Connor is the founder and CEO of White River Design, an award-winning design and branding studio based in Sydney. At the end of 2018, Debbie had a series of work events that left her shattered, deflated and close to breaking point. After reading an article on five signs that you may have burnout she realised she excelled at all five and needed to reach out for help.

Debbie learned that burnout doesn't just happen like a common cold. It's a state of emotional, physical and mental exhaustion caused by excessive and prolonged stress. It occurs when you feel overwhelmed, emotionally drained, and unable to meet constant demands. Adrenal fatigue is the physical result on the body due to excessive stress that leaves you exhausted even when getting sufficient sleep.

But here's the interesting part. Debbie's road to burnout started three and a half years *before* she hit rock bottom. She told me, 'I can see all of the signs with hindsight—working extreme long hours, not asking for help, feeling alone in my quest and disillusioned—but at the time I ignored them, worked harder and tried to soldier on through'. Debbie shared with me how she started withdrawing from her friends and social life, how she seemed to have more negative thoughts than positive and how she felt stuck in her own brain fog, unable to think and second guessing always.

With every day feeling like she was wading through concrete, Debbie was exhausted and overwhelmed, at times nauseous at the thought of going to work. 'Now that I am on the road to recovery I am acutely aware of what to look out for that might trigger a setback.' One year later, Debbie is still recovering. This is the challenge, right? Burnout creeps up on us but it takes years to recover from. Debbie is constantly monitoring her stress levels, her self-care and her downtime. 'Most importantly I am switching my devices off earlier in the evenings and I am actively practising saying "no",' she says.

Extreme exhaustion, the inability to relax and being burnt out is a real threat. It's so real in fact that the World Health Organization re-labelled the syndrome as an 'occupational phenomenon' to better reflect that burnout is a work-based syndrome caused by chronic stress.

A 2018 Gallup study of nearly 7500 full-time employees found that 23 per cent reported feeling burned out at work 'very often' or 'always', while an additional 44 per cent reported feeling burned out 'sometimes'. The report also found that burned-out employees are 63 per cent more likely to take a sick day and 2.6 times as likely to be actively seeking a different job.

Burnout is causing a downward spiral in organisational and individual performance and it's costing us in profits and people. According to a 2019 *Forbes* report:

♦ burnout costs between $125 billion and $190 billion every year in healthcare costs

♦ burnout often leads to disengaged employees, who cost their employers 34 per cent of their annual salary as a result

♦ burnout is responsible for a significant amount of employee turnover, between 20 per cent and 50 per cent or more, depending on the organisation.

Naomi Knight is a corporate strategist and human behaviouralist who has worked in corporate, government and non-government sectors. She says, 'Too many leaders are drowning. Overwhelmed by the enormity of their role, lying awake at 3 am, they feel friendless and hopeless. Stagnating and stuck, organisational performance drops and employee trust in leadership certainty disappears. Unable to make decisions, leader inaction feeds into growing organisational toxicity, compounding uncertainty and silence into failure that degenerates and grows. At this point, there is no leader'.

Acknowledging that extreme exhaustion is kicking in is one thing; doing something about it is another. Authors Melinda Smith, Jeanne Segal and

Lawrence Robinson, in the article 'Burnout prevention and treatment', advise a 'Three Rs' approach:

- *Recognise*: Watch for the warning signs of burnout

- *Reverse*: Undo the damage by seeking support and managing stress

- *Resilience*: Build your resilience to stress by taking care of your physical and emotional health.

As Debbie's story illustrated, it's much harder to come back from burnout than it is to manage and prevent it.

If you're already exhausted with trying to keep up today, how are you going to manage tomorrow?

Law 3: Be Together

Connect with intent

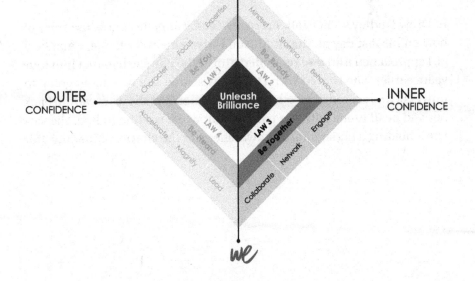

Who do you know? Who knows you?
Engage with others to innovate and ideate.
Connect and collaborate with intent.
Togetherness drives change.

Recently, I was picking up a coffee and I decided to do something a little different.

'Large almond flat white, please,' I said while handing over my 10 dollars. 'And I don't want any change, take it for the next person's coffee.'

When the guy behind me ordered his coffee and was told I had already paid for it, his facial expression moved from 'WTF', to confusion, a gentle smile, then engagement.

'Why would you do that?' he came and asked me.

'Why not?' I said with a smile. 'Happy Monday. Pass it on.'

And at that moment, with that one simple gesture, I knew I'd created a ripple of change for the day — for the guy, for the people around me looking on at the exchange taking place, and hopefully for those who were the recipients of the next 'pass it on'.

Every single thing we say or do makes an impact.

In Drew Dudley's TED Talk *Everyday Leadership*, he shares the story of how on his last day at Mount Allison University in Sackville, Canada, a girl approached him and reminded him of the day she had met him four years earlier. She shared with Drew how scared she was about going to university, so scared in fact that on registration day she was ready to back out and head home with her parents. But while waiting in line, she saw Drew holding a big sign raising awareness for the charity Shinerama (for students fighting cystic fibrosis) and handing out lollipops. Drew turned to the equally nervous guy in the line next to her and said, 'You need to give this lollipop to the beautiful woman next to you'.

She said, 'I felt so bad for the dude that I took the lollipop. As soon as I did, you got this incredibly severe look on your face, looked at my mum and dad and said, "Look at that! Look at that! First day away from home, and already she's taking candy from a stranger!"' Everyone in the line laughed and the tension and fear was defused.

Four years later, the girl shared with Drew that she was still dating that 'dude'. But here's the thing: Drew Dudley doesn't remember that 'lollipop moment', and yet this one single moment had such an incredible impact on the girl's life then and into her future that she wanted to thank him. A year later she sent Drew an invitation to her wedding.

Even though Drew wasn't aware of the impact of this one action, his intentional connection that day made a difference to someone else. He reached out with the aim of relieving unease and tension, and to make someone feel welcome. And this real intent created a connection moment that had a ripple effect of change immediately and over time. Drew argues that the impact we unknowingly have on others, the 'lollipop moments' — these random, everyday moments of true connection — are the ones that create the ripple of change for ourselves and others.

We need to become aware of what we're doing, what we're saying and who we're being every day to ensure we're creating the right impact.

Are you passing on your 'I'm pissed off with my day and everyone in it' message or are you getting out of your own way, acknowledging the impact you can have on the people around you and accepting your responsibility in creating positive ripples?

Togetherness, engaging in the right way, surrounding yourself with the right network of people and collaborating effectively to mutual benefit can be, and is, the only thing that will drive change.

Connecting with intent:

- is not about faking it till you make it

- is not about saying one thing and thinking another

- is not about hiding things from others for fear of being copied

- is not about protection of self or even survival of the fittest

- is certainly not about taking your bad mood out on others.

It's about facing outwards with an interest and willingness to connect and collaborate with others, to exchange value, to care about someone else's success first and to support others' growth. It's about a willingness and desire to embrace the diversity and difference of opinion and ideas, knowing that only by working together, embracing the collective and engaging in the debate, will the ideas and innovations bubble to the surface.

Every time you interact with another person at work or in your life, you have a choice. Do you choose to make it only ever about you and what's in it for you, or do you connect with an intention to listen, to engage, to be curious and to find ways to add value to the conversation or the moment?

The impact of one action (big or small) always has ramifications, one to one, more to more, or many to many.

Make every connection count.

So how do you measure up?

Looking at this diagram, how are you doing?

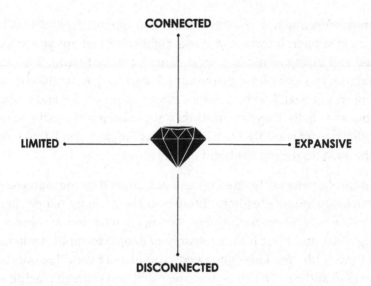

- *Disconnected or connected?* Thinking about your support network professionally and personally, where would you place yourself on the vertical axis of disconnected to connected?

    - Do you feel connected and supported, with an inner circle of people around you?

    - Or do you feel disconnected and without support? Do you feel as if you're going it alone?

- *Limited or expansive?* Now thinking about the horizontal axis of limited to expansive, where would you place yourself?

    - Do you feel encouraged and inspired by the people around you to do more? Are they fuelling and expanding your dreams and pushing you to do more, learn more and become more?

    - Or are you surrounded by people who are limiting your dreams and self-belief, discouraging your actions and destabilising your growth?

Grab a pen and draw an 'X' on the spot that you feel best represents where you're at right now.

You may be feeling like you have incredible support around you, but is it the right support for where you're at right now? Perhaps you're feeling limited and unsupported in your dreams for some reason. You may be feeling like you don't have a sounding board for your thinking as you explore what's next. Maybe there's a bigger game to play and while you may be ready to fly, those around you want to keep you small and boxed into what they're comfortable with. If this is the case, you'll find yourself placing an 'X' in the top left-hand quadrant.

Alternatively, you may be fired up and encouraged by the plan you have for yourself to be more brilliant. There could be a change happening — a new job, a new adventure, a new start-up, a new dream—but you're feeling alone and don't have a network of people to support you at this stage in your life. You know you need to build a network. The question is with whom and how? If this is the case, you'll find yourself placing an 'X' in the bottom right-hand quadrant.

Our ultimate aim is to place ourselves in the top right-hand quadrant. This is a place where we're surrounded by the right people, with the right knowledge and information, who are actively expanding our belief in possibility and encouraging our success. They push us further than we can go ourselves, encourage us to do more and support us every step of the way, firing up our belief and pumping up our 'I can do this'.

The 3 facets of Law 3

Law 3 is where we move from a focus on leading ourselves, to the effective leadership of others.

Leadership expert John C Maxwell summed it up nicely when he said:

> Those closest to you determine your level of success, so choosing the right companions as partners in pursuit of your vision is an important decision. My advice is to surround yourself with talented people who will challenge you, help you grow and inspire you to maximise your potential.

In a world that's moving quicker than ever before we need one another to ideate, to innovate, to work faster and to work smarter. We have to join forces with each other, utilise our collective skills and experience, build connected teams and cultures, and from a place of full disclosure and confidence, share insights, perspectives and thoughts openly.

As Keith Ferrazzi concludes in *Never Eat Alone*, 'Success in life = (the people you meet) + (what you create together)'.

Law 3 requires a focus on these three facets:

- Engage
- Network
- Collaborate.

So, let's go!

Facet 7

Engage

In a recent Gallup article, Jennifer Robison explains that millennials like to job-hop because only 29 per cent are engaged at work. Robison says they continually search for high-quality management that provides opportunities to learn and grow and to do work that's purposeful.

Now I'm not convinced that this need for increased engagement at work is only reserved for those born post 1981! All of us, of all ages, are seeking connection with others and the opportunity to learn and better ourselves.

We all crave to be engaged and excited by our work within teams, with our clients and with each other.

CEOs approach me at the end of year-long leadership programs and say, 'Wow the team are so connected and engaged. There's so much support in this room for each other — how did you do that?' My answer is, 'I care about their success. I want them to succeed and the only way to do this is to respect and get to know each individual by creating a safe space where we can talk and engage. I choose to listen, to really listen, because how can I truly provide help and support if I don't understand where they're currently at?'

People ask me, 'How do I network? What's the first thing I should say?' My answer is always, 'Say hi, be yourself and talk. Be truly interested in the other person and ask them a question. Listen carefully and then ask another question'.

Years later I bump into people I met at conferences, whom I trained or mentored, and I'll remember something about them — not just what they do — and people ask me how I do that. Again, it's because I'm interested in people, in getting to know something about them.

These are just examples to illustrate that ...

... engagement is about connecting and being truly interested in getting to know the other person — it's that simple.

I often say to my clients, 'I know more about your people than you do' (sad, but true!). You may know their career aspirations (though, sometimes, I'm not convinced that's the case), you know what their capability and performance score is and what you think is going on for them, but I reckon I know more about them than you do. I know what's going on for them personally, what challenges they're really having at work, their belief systems, their fears and limitations, their hopes and dreams. Why? Because I make an effort to connect and engage first and foremost. This is how I push people out of their comfort zone and to a new frontier of competence.

Every single one of us is so much more than our job titles, salaries, the cars we drive and where we live. Building engagement is as simple as being curious and interested in the other person, in what's going on for them, and meeting them where they're at. It's about having a conversation with the whole person — not just the job they do and where they work.

It doesn't matter whether you're a leader or an employee, a celebrity or a fan, a parent or a child, engagement across boundaries is all about meeting people where they're at, getting curious, finding a connection point and moving forward together.

Challenge your assumptions

Ron Harvey is a retired US army veteran based in Columbia, South Carolina. He is now a certified coach as part of the John Maxwell team, and we met studying together at Harvard Kennedy School in early 2019.

Returning home from deployment in the Gulf War at the age of 26, Ron was selected for recruitment duty and assigned to a city called Davie in Florida. He was recruiting a young Caucasian man and drove out to meet his family in full uniform. When Ron got to the house, the young man's mother opened the door and said, 'You can work with my son, but you can't come in. I don't let black people in my house'.

Ron was naturally angry and hurt as the discrimination hit him hard. 'The most difficult thing for me was I wasn't even respected in the country that I had fought for, where I had experienced loss of life, and had put my own life in jeopardy. The fact that my race was the reason why I wasn't respected — that was the most difficult thing.'

Ron knew that the decision he made next about how to engage with the mother would change the trajectory for the young man, for himself, for the other African-American recruiters and for anybody of any race for that matter.

Recalling the story, he says, 'I gathered myself really quickly. I told her I'm sorry she feels that way and I said I would be more than happy to talk to her son in the car'.

In the car, the son got angry. He was frustrated and embarrassed at the situation and started speaking disrespectfully about his mother. Ron told me 'the military doesn't believe in disrespecting authority. Whether right or wrong, being respectful is critical,' and so he told the mother that the army wasn't as interested in her son as initially thought because they believe in respecting authority. 'His disrespect for you will cause problems for us,' said Ron. Ron didn't do the interview that day.

The young man did eventually enter the army, but it's what the mother did next that illustrates the power of engagement.

She called Ron on Easter Sunday and told him her son had shown a high level of respect for Ron, and that this was the first time he'd really respected someone at that level of authority. She had witnessed how Ron had engaged with her son and helped change his world view.

She invited Ron to her house to apologise. She shared how she'd been raised and how this had affected her own belief system and racial judgement. From witnessing Ron's engagement with her son and how this had changed him, she shared that her own belief system and judgement around race were challenged. She wanted to learn more from Ron — to engage. She said that she was willing to challenge her learnt beliefs and renegotiate what these meant for her moving forward. She had to be brave enough to unlearn and relearn. Ron welcomed the conversation with open arms and with no judgement and he and this mother have subsequently stayed in contact, sharing many a conversation over a meal at her house.

Ron's story of racial discrimination, his acceptance and love for people and his powerful poise in the moment — as well as his open vulnerability around his anger at being judged not on how he'd served his country but on the colour of his skin — moved me and the rest of the Harvard class to tears.

In his learning he shared that 'people are insecure and not willing to listen because of the fear they may learn something. Even for that mother, at that moment when she saw me, she wasn't willing to listen. But as she listened to her son later, and saw that he cared and that I was someone who was going to help her son achieve something that she wanted him to achieve, she found herself in a position where she needed to listen and she needed my help'.

Ron's story is an example of the opportunity that exists when we're willing and prepared to meet people where they're at. When we're brave enough to connect and be emotionally involved and fully committed to the conversation. When we're willing to listen and when we want to learn to understand.

Engaging in the right way is about being okay with being challenged about our own existing beliefs, to rethink original thoughts, to be comfortable in the space of being proved wrong.

It's about willingly engaging with diversity of thought, opinion, culture and experience versus sitting comfortably only among those who think, believe and behave just like you.

It's about acceptance. It's about debate, agreement and disagreement. It's about knowing that only by engaging and coming together are we creating an opportunity to drive collective momentum.

> **Engaging with others is a willingness to be interested and choosing to understand and appreciate others without judgement.**

Ron's willingness to engage with someone whose belief system upset and angered him, knowing that this engagement had the potential for many knock-on ramifications to the mother, the son, the wider family, the community and his comrades, illustrates a willingness to be curious, to appreciate, to not judge but to explore more deeply. To ask, 'I wonder what's going on?', to ultimately love unconditionally and be willing to hear and understand someone else's perspective and point of view.

Imagine what the world could be like if there were more Rons in it?

Imagine what your world could be like if you were prepared to suspend judgement and, in its place, engage deeply to move forward with others.

Heart, not head

In 1938, Harvard University began following 724 participants as part of the longest running study on human development in history. The study was developed to determine what makes us happy. The study explored every part of who we are—from physical and psychological traits to social life and IQ — to learn how we can flourish. Findings were published in the 2012 book *Triumphs of Experience*, with key results showing that happiness and health aren't a result of wealth, fame or working hard, but come instead from our relationships with each other.

The positive impact of strong engagement levels was further reinforced in the findings of a 2018 report. Researchers explored how social support influences university students' academic achievement and concluded that the more a person felt they were supported, the better their self-esteem and their performance. The research team suggested that social support and self-esteem work in a sort of 'feedback loop', with one bolstering the other.

The benefits of social engagement and good mental health are numerous. Proven links include lower rates of anxiety and depression, higher self-esteem, greater empathy, and more trusting and cooperative relationships. Strong, healthy relationships can also help to strengthen your immune system, help you recover from disease and may even lengthen your life.

When we have stronger ties and a sense of purpose, our happiness levels are fuelled. We:

- create a positive workplace
- are willing to put in the extra effort
- treat each other with respect and acceptance
- are more productive and successful
- are more innovative, thinking outside the box, and curious about how we can improve and do better.

To increase engagement levels across the board, we need to practise how we engage individually, human to human, and heart to heart.

We need to practise connecting with intent, which requires:

- *being present and in the moment*: focusing on the other person — we always remember how people make us feel

- *being interested*: listening deeply, developing understanding and broadening perspective — we feel valued and respected when others are interested in us and our thoughts and opinions

- *giving praise and encouragement*: we feel hope when others make us feel great about ourselves or help us find perspective

- *committing to operating from a place of 'we'*: we feel connected when we feel like we're in it together

- *being enthusiastic and having fun*: we build our strongest relationships when we laugh and have fun

- *engaging in two-way conversations*: sharing value with each other.

At the end of the day, business has been and always will be about people. Leadership is and always has been about meeting people where they're at, paving the path to a new future and creating a desire to collectively work in the direction you're envisioning.

Discussion, debate, ideas and innovation need us, together, to engage. Support, help, solution finding and compassion only happen when we truly work together, when we engage and when we ultimately start re-engaging as people first and foremost.

And this also means banning the bullshit!

Ban the BS

We waste so much time and energy hiding behind the stories we tell ourselves, the external personal brand we want to present to the world, that we engage with the head and totally avoid the heart. We're not engaging, but rather faking it till we make it. We all have an incredible nose for the bullshit in others — and others can sense the BS in us!

According to Lewis Howes, *New York Times* best-selling author of *The School of Greatness*, people can tell when others aren't being real, and to become more likeable and personable you should focus on developing genuine connections, and not on what others can do for you. He maintains that in business, this may not be required to be a great leader, but it will make you a respected leader.

The crazy thing is that we're living in a world where we're able to engage and connect more than ever before: mobile phone, the internet, instant messaging, social media. Millions of people are chatting, sharing and creating around the world at the same time, and new data, information, news and ideas reach us at the click of a button. Yet this just adds to the bullshit!

There's a lot of 'telling' going on, a one-way blasting out of information and facts. We can research the living daylights out of anything online, consume content in a multitude of formats and receive notifications, should we choose, every second of every day. We're able to check in with friends from around the world daily via short, succinct conversations, selfies and holiday posts. We can choose to engage in serious online debates and discussions, or stalk others secretly from behind a computer screen, and we all love the frivolous conversations and cat memes that give us a giggle. This is merely an information exchange — and it's dangerous.

You have to engage as *you*, not as some wonderfully coiffured, perfectly polished, edited and retouched version of you. We want to get to know you and all your uncomfortable, jiggly bits. Otherwise, you may as well print off that retouched selfie picture from your Instagram feed and pop up a cardboard cut-out of yourself instead!

Ask yourself honestly, how well are you showing up? Go on, be honest with yourself: is there some BS that you're sharing right now? Or are you just presenting the perfectly polished version of you?

In what ways could you remove the BS and be a more real version of yourself?

Make every moment count

Dr Michael Perry is a retired army lieutenant colonel with 20 years of service, and now co-founder and COO of Catalyst Executive Advising & Development where he and his team focus on developing leaders with the courage and vision to transform culture and change lives. I met Dr Perry during a trip to the United States.

It was during an interview with him that he shared the story of being in his office working when his daughter walked in to have a conversation. He remembers listening to his daughter, but not really listening as he had his back turned to her and was typing at his computer while she was talking (I don't think he's the only one who has done this, right?!).

He said, 'Suddenly, I realised with the busyness of work, I was neglecting the thing that was the most important'. In that moment of distraction, Dr Perry shares how he lost the opportunity to engage with his daughter and instead chose to engage with the work. He realised this had to change if he was going to build a strong relationship with his daughter, asking himself, 'How many moments have I missed because I've been so enthralled in what I was doing that I was distracted from what was going on in that moment?'

I'm sure many of us can relate to this battle between intention and distraction as we spend our lives juggling multiple balls and demands on our time. Equally, I wonder how many moments we're missing with our clients, staff, customers, family and friends. How often the answers are right there in front of us, but in our busyness and race through life the clues in the moment disappear into the ether.

Dr Perry shared that engagement matters no matter who you're talking to and this requires work and focus on our part. He says, 'They deserve everything I have at that moment. Because if I'm giving a portion of myself to anything else, then I'm doing that particular thing or person a disservice'.

How connected, present and engaged are you really?

How many moments are you missing and what's the detrimental impact of that?

Open your eyes

A few years ago, I was working with a senior IT executive. She was well respected, results oriented and on a fast-track to promotion. During one of our sessions she angrily shared with me her frustration about a member of her team who used to be a high achiever but for some reason his performance had gone off the boil in the previous few weeks. It didn't matter what she did in terms of one-on-one conversation — helping with priorities, setting short-term goals — nothing helped. Her only solution, she told me, was to go to HR and start the process of performance discussion.

'Have you actually asked him what's going on?' I asked.

'Yeah, yeah, sort of. He says he's got a lot on his plate, that he's trying, but quite frankly I need his performance to improve and it's not good enough right now,' was her response.

'But he used to be one of your best performers, correct?' I replied.

'Yes, but not anymore and nothing seems to be improving.'

So instead of finding out what was going on, my client had started performance proceedings with HR!

I suggested, irrespective of where they were at in the company HR process, she needed to sit down and have a deeper conversation. What was *really* going on?

And to her credit she did.

She discovered that both his parents were sick in the UK, he was worrying about them and this worry for his family was all-consuming, taking over from any focus or interest he had in his work or the business. Quite rightly, his sick parents were his priority.

Here's the thing though: because of the formal HR proceedings, he'd lost all loyalty to the company and ended up resigning.

This story could have ended so much better: granting extended leave, carer support programs. But no, instead she chose to let process and protocol sort it out.

This is a classic example of being so wrapped up in the surface-level tasks of getting the job done, of self, that you're totally disengaged and blind to the other person.

Another time I was mentoring a senior executive for a large serviced office in Queensland. He was killing it on the results front — the figures were great, projects were being ticked off — but he felt his team were not being a team.

'When was the last time you had a good conversation with them, individually? To find out what's going on outside of work?'

He shared that team meetings happened every week, one-on-one catch ups were in the diary and that team social outings were scheduled somewhere in the 12-month plan.

'Yeah, yeah, I get that. But do you really know your team?'

After a blank response I challenged him for two weeks to engage individually with every member of his team and to have a conversation that didn't involve work, task lists or project plans. To actually engage, to find out about his team: their lives and what makes them tick.

Two weeks later he came back more excited than I'd experienced in any previous meeting. He began to reel off the stories he'd discovered: how one employee looked after his sick mother, how another was doing a yoga training course, how another volunteered at a local charity and how another was planning to ask his girlfriend to get married.

'Awesome,' I said. 'How does all this information make you feel and what are you going to do next?'

He proceeded to share how he felt more engaged with his team, how he had developed a greater understanding of their interests and key drivers and how, by having conversations that involved more than work, he felt more connected to his team.

The risk we all take is that we spend too much time with our eyes down looking at our screens or the immediate work at hand. We live in our heads; among our spreadsheets, project plans and sales targets. We get lost in the noise of our email inbox. We're racing through life and our days, just existing and oblivious to what's going on around us.

We're failing to stop and take notice of the clues that people are giving us: the employee who's no longer engaging in meetings, the partner whose shoulders are slumped as they trudge in from work, the child who's quietly sitting in their room night after night.

And if we do notice these things, we seem to actively avoid any person-to-person contact, worrying about what to say, how to say it, and we may jump into process mapping a solution, the protocol of correcting in the right way or the 'seven steps to sorting it out', instead of stopping and being curious — instead of engaging, human to human.

Engagement is about creating the space to allow others to be themselves, to be imperfect and free to make mistakes. Engagement is about creating the space for both parties to share their inherent humanity, their dreams and aspirations, their passions and their lives in their entirety, knowing that togetherness is the one opportunity to drive change for each other.

When was the last time you actually stopped, chatted and connected over more than calendar commitments and project plans?

Take a moment to think about how you could engage more with the people you work with and the people at home.

What could you start doing this week to deepen the relationships you already have?

Trust builds engagement

While on holidays in Hawaii, the ride-share app Uber became my family's go-to. Onto the app we'd jump, load our trip details and accept the allocated ride, essentially placing our trust in the driver to get us safely to our destination. On the same holiday, we'd use the app OpenTable to find the best restaurants in the area based on ratings, reviews and the recommendations of others.

Yet isn't it interesting, that as much as we put our trust in websites and apps, and complete strangers who rate our experiences or drive our cars, as a society we're extremely distrusting of companies, brands, businesses and government?

The 2018 Edelman Trust Barometer describes it as 'a world of seemingly stagnant distrust'. According to this report, our trust in business, governments, media and brands is at an all-time low. The same report also identifies that nearly seven in 10 respondents believe building trust is the number one job for CEOs, ahead of high-quality products and services.

Trust is a vital feature of human interaction and a fundamental building block for engagement and connecting with intent. The high value of trust is linked to its scarcity. It takes time to develop as each small step and behaviour contributes to the building of trust. And just as it takes time to build trust, it only takes one small event or behaviour to diminish or destroy it completely and you're back to square one.

In a research report titled 'Why trust is critical to team success', Dennis and Michelle Reina and David Hudnut stated that,

> *When trust is present, people step forward and do their best work, together, efficiently. They align around a common purpose, take risks, think out of the box, have each other's backs, and communicate openly and honestly.*

However, they continued, when there's no trust people manipulate others, hide information, don't take risks and talk about, rather than to, others.

Trust is a two-way street. We have to give trust to receive trust. In her book *Dare to Lead*, Brené Brown introduced BRAVING trust, with the acronym standing for:

◆ *Boundaries* — I will trust you if you hold and respect boundaries

◆ *Reliability* — I will trust you if you do what you say you're going to do

◆ *Accountability* — I will trust you if you own your mistakes, apologise and make amends, and I will do the same

◆ *Vault* — I will trust you if you hold what I share in confidence

◆ *Integrity* — I will trust you if you choose courage over comfort; choose what's right rather than what's quick and enjoyable; and practise, not just speak, your values

◆ *Non-judgement* — I will trust you if you accept who I am and what I'm telling you without judgement

◆ *Generosity* — I will trust you if you'll make a generous assumption for me.

To build trust with others, you have to learn to brave trust so others can trust you too. You have to be brave enough to connect your head with your heart; to meet others and engage where they're at.

People will follow you, work hard for you, support you, even maybe make their own sacrifices for you, if they trust you and feel connected to you.

Brilliance in action

1. Get curious

Take a moment to think about your team or the people you work with. How much do you really know about them? Think past their performance at work and what they've shared about their 'what's next'. What else do you know? If the answer is, 'mmm, not much', what can you do to deepen the relationship? Why not take on the challenge I set one of my clients: for two weeks speak to your team about anything other than work and see what you can find out.

2. Brave trust

Take a look at Brené Brown's BRAVING acronym. Where are you performing well and where do you think you can make improvements? What are you noticing about yourself? What are you going to commit to changing?

Facet 8

Network

In 2010, I was working full-time as Group Marketing Director for Oroton Group, Australia & New Zealand, looking after the Oroton and Ralph Lauren brands. My professional life looked glamorous, at least on paper. It was jammed with fashion shoots, invitations to international fashion weeks, store opening events and media parties. Yet personally, my husband and I were juggling full-time jobs with three children under seven and all that comes with that.

Life was frantic, to say the least, and I felt like I was constantly giving to others and giving nothing to myself. My days were spent giving to my team, media, clients and suppliers, and reporting back to the fabulous Ralph Lauren team in New York. I felt drained. Everything revolved around industry-specific, sometimes superficial, surface-level chit-chat or conversations about managing mother guilt and how to chase the infamous work–life balance.

As much as I was enjoying all I was doing, I felt lonely and disconnected. I didn't have like-minded people around me I could talk to about current challenges, big-picture thinking or decisions I had to make, and I certainly didn't feel like I was feeding my brain. I was existing (albeit not very well at times) rather than being.

I remember one evening thinking to myself that there must be other women out there like me. Women who wanted to keep growing and developing their thinking and mastery. Women who wanted to build personal success as well as nurture a family and friends. Women who wanted to keep achieving more.

And so, one day I decided I was going to host a private dinner to fulfil my need for great connection and smart, deep conversation. I reached out to eight Sydney-based businesswomen I respected and admired and invited them to join me for dinner.

At this dinner we talked about successes and challenges. We debated future thinking. It felt amazing to have smart conversations with savvy business leaders. My heart and mind were full of support, understanding and new ideas to think about. And I wasn't the only one to feel this way. At the end of this dinner I was asked if I could host another dinner and if they could extend the invitation to a friend.

Over the course of the next few months I hosted more and more dinners. The networks forming were incredible as we realised that we're all exactly the same, facing our own personal and professional challenges with the desire to drive commercial success for ourselves and each other.

After a fair bit of number crunching, soul searching and asking myself 'What if?, 'Could I?' and 'Is this possible?' I decided to leave my full-time corporate career, put on my big girl pants and bootstrap my own networking business. In June 2011, on my 40th birthday, I officially launched the LBDGroup as a membership-based business. Yes, I was absolutely petrified. Yes, I was fearful about making the wrong decision. But I also knew I had to give it a go. The evidence and demand were there — it was more about whether I was brave enough to step through the door and try.

Over the next eight years the LBDGroup grew from strength to strength, launching nationally across Australia and testing the platform in London and Singapore. We hosted monthly networking dinners, think tanks, conferences, retreats and learning webinars, and extended our impact philanthropically through the development of the First Seeds Fund, a gift-giving circle committed to supporting women and children at the grass roots of Australia.

I really love this quote from Brené Brown as I think it sums up the essence of the LBDGroup: 'Live-tweeting your bikini wax is not vulnerability. Nor is posting a blow-by-blow of your divorce. That's an attempt to hot-wire connection. But you can't cheat real connection. It's built up slowly. It's about trust and time.'

Networking is more than handing out business cards, superficial shallow business conversation, the well-rehearsed elevator pitch or learning the 'seven easy steps'.

I feel truly blessed to have met all the amazing women who have been part of LBDGroup (which I've since sold) and doubly blessed that so many continue to be part of my world. I smile deeply when I see connection and collaboration still having its ripple effect even after all these years, and I'm truly excited to support and watch the next phase of LBDGroup as it continues to evolve and grow.

This is the power of networking the right way. As Desmond Tutu so rightly said, 'A person is a person through other persons; you can't be human in isolation, you are human only in relationships'.

Connect and be human

One of the first questions I ask during my keynotes or training sessions is, 'So how many of you love networking?' And I reckon on average only 5–10 per cent of the room will put their hand up.

The rest would rather hide under the table at events, avoiding conversation or eye contact — or even more likely, stay home doing something they find much more fun than meeting and chatting to strangers. Most of them will cite disliking the superficial conversation, a feeling of being sold to or the fakeness of the situation.

There's no doubt that many of us feel:

1. networking is a chore

2. networking is something people have to do when they want something: that new job, that business lead, that advice.

Networking needs a reframe because it is, ultimately, all about connection. Connection is about being yourself. And being yourself is about being human.

And yet we appear to be living in an age of extremes. On the one hand obsessing about the quantity of 'friends', connections and the size of the databases we're trying to build. On the other, struggling with the busyness of life and keeping in touch with said 'friends'.

We're suffering with a deficiency of time to pay any depth of attention to anything. Often, time is spread so thinly that the depth of connection is not deep at all; surface level conversations and discussions become as normal as a debate about the weekend's weather, and we're so caught up in quantity that we forget that the best things do, in fact, come in small packages.

In this world of disconnection, we all have to slow down to initiate deeper connection with each other.

Everyone needs a network. It doesn't matter what you do, what level you operate on, what industry you're in, or whether you work for an organisation or are out on your own.

So how do we network in a way that feeds our hearts and our minds?

How do we build connections that really matter so that we feel connected and supported — so that we can leverage who we are to become and all we want to be?

How do we do it in a way that's more than the transactional swapping of business cards, the click of a 'like' button or an 'add' to the mailing list?

First, you need to unlearn everything you've been told to date about networking and ask yourself:

- Who is in my network now?

- Who should be in my network now?

- How can we work *together* as a group to effect change?

Building a network for personal brilliance is about:

- connecting and collaborating with the right people

- openly sharing knowledge and insights with individuals who understand, at a deeper level, our goals and aspirations

- knowing that when we learn to move together we start to move faster.

We need to find, develop and nurture the right network to become more brilliant today and even more brilliant tomorrow.

Be intentional

Kara Atkinson is the founder and CEO of SPARC | The Sales Leader Network and The Sales Recruiter. She first connected with me over a love of books.

'I'm an avid consumer of business books and have three to four on the go at any one time,' she said. 'I love to get to the guts of a book quickly so there aren't many I can think of that I've completely consumed beginning to end, but I was gifted your book, *It's Who You Know* at a conference. I thought I knew everything about networking. I mean, I've got more than 10 000 LinkedIn connections for starters, so I flippantly leafed through it before I read the introduction. When I saw your claim that you only need 12 people in your network to create real influence and impact, it stopped me dead! I cancelled my dinner plans and read the book cover to cover. It blew my mind.

'After a night spent stalking you online, I was surprised to bump into you at the conference the next day. I stuck my hand out and said, "Hi, you don't know me, but I think we need to be in each other's life".'

Fast-forward two years, and Kara and I still work, and still socialise, together and Kara's recruitment company has tripled in size. But better than that, Kara realised that her 20-year-plus headhunting business had to evolve from the commodity and transactions facilitated by her industry. Connecting with intent to create long-lasting relationships is the heart of everything she now does. It has led her to create and found SPARC | The Sales Leader Network, the only global network exclusively for sales leaders. It's a safe space where sales leaders can have a blood-on-the-wall conversation with no ramifications, a place where they can learn and challenge their thinking. Ultimately, at the heart of this network is collaboration and a genuine desire to see others soar.

Kara's story demonstrates the power of connecting with intent and now she's passing this know-how on to create an opportunity for others to experience the same. There's no doubt in my mind that connecting with intent matters — for you and for those you connect with.

Networking the right way requires interest in others and a curiosity to explore what magic can be created together. It's about putting yourself in someone else's world and getting curious about what you can do to help first and foremost. It's about putting others' success and career above your own, focusing on what you can give and nurturing the value in the relationship.

So how well are you connecting with intent right now?

Are you just spraying out LinkedIn connections and hoping for the best? Or are you putting yourself out there, being curious about opportunities to connect with people on a deeper level?

Your inner circle

At the 2019 Australian Open Novak Djokovic won the men's singles title for a record-breaking seventh time. In his acceptance speech he talked to the fact that a year earlier he'd been undergoing surgery and that without the collective effort of his team he couldn't have achieved this title. He thanked his coaching team one by one for developing the formula for him that's working, and he thanked his inner circle, his family, for their unparalleled support through tough times.

In my previous book, *It's Who You Know,* I share that we really only need 12 key people (not 1200!) to drive and support our success. I developed and tested this framework on the back of research and many, many, interviews with successful thought leaders, consultants, leaders and more. I examined how people manage their corporate careers, how they maintained relationships as they moved companies and countries and how they build solid, deep and long-lasting connections. Connections that inspire, share, add value, encourage and motivate. Connections that transform.

Since publishing that book in 2017, I've spoken, trained and mentored thousands of individuals around the world in this thinking around strategically building a network of 'you' to support your professional and personal growth and success. I've helped vice presidents of technology companies use the framework to find their next role after being made redundant after 20 years with a company; CEOs develop their support team at a new company; founders of start-ups develop their network to help get their idea off the ground; introverted executives achieve their next career move; CMOs and property executives get the job of their dreams overseas; and executives move to senior roles.

This powerful network of *you* is more than a pocketful of business cards, a database full of contacts, a list of 'friends' on social media (all of which I accept are needed for lead generation and business growth).

Rather, your key 12 add an additional powerful layer of awesomeness to you. They understand you, your goals and your dreams for success. They respect your strengths and your imperfections, the areas you rock at and the areas you need support in. They provide quality thinking and behaviours, and push you further than you could ever go alone.

Your inner circle has to evolve over time as you continually initiate new connections aligned to your current business or personal needs. It needs to be diverse, cross-functional and boundary spanning, providing critical insight, ideation, thought and opinion to challenge and add to your existing thinking.

The key 12 people I share as part of the 'it's who you know' networking framework are categorised into four groups, and you really need just one person in each of the four groups to begin with.

1. Promoters

These are the people who will help you achieve more, the individuals who always see more in you than you see in yourself. They see possibility where you see impossibility. They're a cheerleader, an explorer and an inspirer. Your own personal cheerleading squad. They're with you by your side through thick or thin, never giving up on you, always dreaming big with you. Promoters pull you towards your future dreams, make noise about potential possibilities, spend time with you to explore how you're going to achieve your goals and inspire you to become more.

Need more proof? According to research from the Center for Talent Innovation, people with promoters (aka sponsors) are 23 per cent more likely to move up in their career than those without sponsors. In addition, a 2011 study from the Center for Work-Life Policy published by the *Harvard Business Review* found that active promotion of others can result in as much as a 30 per cent increase in promotions, pay rises and projects for the person being sponsored.

So, who's flying your flag right now?

Who's helping promote you?

2. Pit crew

Climbing the success ladder can be a lonely task. The journey requires grit, determination and perseverance. We all experience days of frustration and disappointment, days when we have to face our fears, make tough decisions, push past failures and keep focused on opportunities that lie outside our comfort zone.

Your pit crew doesn't care about what you do, how much money you earn or any of the materialistic trappings of success. They care about you. They're there to help keep you mentally tough and balanced, your feet on the ground, and your mental and physical health in check.

Like a Formula One pit stop, your pit crew can make or break a race. They add stamina to run the marathon of your dreams, to navigate complexities and recover from setbacks. They help you learn from mistakes and keep pushing you on. They celebrate your wins, remind you of your achievements and keep it real.

Who would you say you have in your network now looking out for you?

Who celebrates the highs and catches you when you fall?

3. Teachers

A life of continuous learning is essential to growth. Successful people know this; that's why they have an insatiable desire and commitment to learn more, in more ways than one.

Harvard professor Linda Hill says, 'You can't think of something new unless you are being pushed to think in new directions, and you can't do that unless you are engaging with people who have a different viewpoint'.

The right teachers teach you mastery, guide and stretch your thinking, challenge your ideas, and encourage you to push further because they know that this constant curiosity creates real opportunity for growth, achievement and success. They're an architect, a professor and an influencer. They may have been there and done that too but will ultimately be someone you're learning from.

Do you have a teacher in your inner circle who's stretching and challenging your thinking?

If not, is there someone you admire who you could reach out to and connect with?

4. Butt-kickers

Love them or hate them, we all need butt-kickers: those individuals who help accelerate the journey, pushing you to do more and holding you accountable for all your actions. They accelerate action, they mentor you through your thinking and decision making and they call you on your bullshit.

Butt-kickers are masters of delivery. They hold you accountable for your actions and decisions, and ensure you do what you say you're going to do — and then some. Your butt-kicker is like a personal trainer. They count your push-ups and pull-ups, and they always make you do one extra for good measure.

Linda Galindo, author of *The 85% Solution*, believes butt-kickers are our secret weapon to success. 'Working with a partner prevents the ready-fire-aim approach that a lot of entrepreneurs use.'

Who's kicking your butt?

Who helps you follow through on the commitments you make to yourself?

Surrounding yourself with the right people like this is key to your success.

Fly with eagles

When Carter, my youngest son, was 11 he had to do some research for a school project on eagles, and we discovered that they actually love storms.

Apparently when clouds gather, eagles get excited. They use the raging storm winds to lift and fly higher, giving them an opportunity to glide and rest their wings.

In the meantime, all the other birds hide in the leaves and branches of the trees — some loudly chirping at the impending storm; others staying quiet, hiding, protecting themselves, staying safe.

What do you do when a proverbial storm hits?

Do you calmly rise above the storm with fellow eagles, gliding and navigating through the various challenges with the ultimate aim of reaching the desired end goal? Or do you bunker down alone and attempt to work out problems in isolation? Or do you choose to hide as a collective in the proverbial branches, chittering and chattering about all the issues, creating dramas, debating options but not really moving anywhere as you wait for the storm to pass, handing over decision making to others?

The reality is that life and work aren't all champagne and unicorns (as much as I wish they were). There are moments when the shit well and truly hits the fan, and this is when you have to pull on the people around you to support, guide and encourage you through to the other side of the storm.

Emma Isaacs is the founder and global CEO of Business Chicks. She has grown this phenomenal community from a group of around 250 members to a global business that runs across two continents and 11 cities, produces more than 100 events annually and reaches more than 500 000 women.

But it was Emma's first attempt to take Business Chicks into the United States where she had to really pull on the support of her fellow eagles.

After building a phenomenal business footprint in Australia, Emma decided it was time to launch the Business Chicks business into the American market. She packed up her home and family and moved to Los Angeles.

The Business Chicks brand well and truly resonated as Emma and her team successfully pulled off large-scale events with over 700 people flocking to fill ballrooms in Los Angeles, New York and San Francisco. But the actual cost of running events in the United States was under-estimated. 'And the end result was that we'd lose a bunch of money each time,' Emma shared with me during an interview for my podcast. She added, 'The upshot is that our launch into the United States was pretty much a complete failure. It cost me close to $2 million. It caused a lot of stress to my family, and to my leadership team in Australia'.

Finally, Emma and her team made the tough decision to stop running the business in the United States and to put plans on hold. 'That time was terrible,' shared Emma. 'To be really honest, that was my first really big business failure. I've had a tonne of failures, but none that cost as much, and none that hurt as deeply as that.'

During the ordeal Emma reached out to her network and fellow eagles for advice. In her bestselling book, *Winging It*, Emma shares that one person she confided in was Richard Branson. 'He was comforting and helped put it all in perspective for me, mentioning a bunch of his business disasters, such as Virgin Cola and another couple I'd never heard of before.'

Emma explained that she has attracted into her orbit, people who understand the entrepreneurial mentality, and what it actually takes to grow and run businesses.

'We're there for each other in the moments, and you can condense that into a 10-minute conversation rather than having to have a three-hour coffee. It's like, "What do you need? What's going on? Tell me". A quick coaching kind of conversation.'

When Emma's storm hit she needed her circle of proverbial eagles to help her navigate the possible options ahead and to help with decision making.

Who are the eagles in your world?

It's not about hiding or playing safe. It's about embracing the power of a collective. It's about you choosing to surround yourself with eagles — individuals who may have already walked the path you're walking, who want to see you succeed — because together you can fly so much higher than you would ever fly alone.

So, who are the eagles around you who are complementing and adding to your goals and dreams, your skills and your leadership?

Who are the people who will carefully help you ride that storm to ultimately fly above it and move forward?

Reach out

We often think that seeking out these people means we have to attend networking events and do the equivalent of 'cold calling'. Nothing could be further from the truth.

Your eagles are closer than you think. They're already encouraging you to do more, feeding you information and smarts, checking in on your progress and how you're tracking or even holding you accountable to your goals on a daily, weekly or monthly basis. Open your eyes and ears because your network is right in front of you. And here's the thing: even if you still can't identify them, the people you already respect and admire are likely to know someone you should meet. You simply have to be brave enough to reach out.

I've lost count of how many times I've been asked, 'How do I approach (insert name)? What do I say?'

My answer is:

1.   Get clear on the *one question* you want to ask.

2.   Ask them the question! Seriously, it's as simple as that.

This first element, the *one* question, is so important (and always overlooked). We absolutely have to respect other people's time. So, don't just ask them for 'a coffee to pick their brain'. Don't just ask them to be 'part of your network'. And don't send them a long list of questions via LinkedIn (ugh).

Be direct; be thoughtful about what you're seeking.

If you really value someone's opinion and advice, then invest your time first to get clear on what help you need. Get specific in your request and I guarantee most people will be willing to help, and if they can't, they're very likely to respond with an explanation or even introduce you to someone who would be better at helping with said advice.

As opposed to 'Can I meet you for a coffee?' (which is a sure-fire sign that you're going to chew up their precious time) say, 'I'd like to chat with you about the three key things you did to grow your career to becoming a partner' or 'I'm looking to expand into China and noticed you had managed to do so successfully. I'd really appreciate it if you could share your three key insights' or 'I've been following you on social media and love what you're doing. What is the one key tip you would share?'

Show you're interested. Show you care. Show that you've invested your own time thinking about the key question or piece of advice you want to ask about.

Then, when you finally connect, be present and ask your one question. Listen to what they're saying, engage in conversation. Take notes, gather intelligence, be diligent, commit to taking action and make sure to say thank you. You could even follow up with a handwritten card and state the action you'll be taking immediately.

I realise this is common sense, but you would not believe how many people seem to forget this basic etiquette! Remember that you initiated the original conversation, which was the catalyst for opportunity and opened up the possibility of forming a longer-term relationship.

Own it. Be curious. Be brave. Reach out — and don't forget to expect the unexpected.

Give and take

In his book *Give and Take*, Adam Grant suggests the individuals most likely to rise to the top are often 'Givers', those who contribute most to others. 'Takers', who seek to gain as much as possible from others, and 'Matchers', who aim to give and take in equal amounts, rarely experience the same success. In addition, something magical happens when 'Givers' thrive.

Givers succeed in a way that creates a ripple effect, enhancing the success of people around them. Every time we interact with another person at work, we have a choice to make: do we try to claim as much value as we can, or contribute value without worrying about what we receive in return?

Value exchange is about two or more individuals sharing insights, connections, knowledge and ideas. Value exchange is like throwing a pebble into a pond. Individually we're all capable of creating some kind of movement, but working together we create ripples that build momentum and impact as they spread.

It's time to stop network transacting and, in its place, build transformative human connections. Invest time and energy into exchanging value mutually because on the other side of this investment lie trust, depth of understanding, connected visions and the achievement of goals.

Above all else, remember:

♦ Networking is connecting.

♦ Connecting is being yourself.

♦ Being yourself is being human.

Brilliance in action

1. Identify your inner circle

Thinking about the goals you have for yourself over the next 12 months, who is your promoter, pit crew, teacher and butt-kicker?

Think about who you already know, and if there's a gap, consider who you'd like to reach out to and why.

	WHO I already know	WHO I would like to know	WHY do I want to know this person?
Promoter			
Pit crew			
Teacher			
Butt-kicker			

(continued)

Brilliance in action (*cont'd*)

2. Fill the gaps

Get clear on why you want to meet someone. What's the one question you'd like to ask? How are you going to reach out—for example, ask for an introduction from someone you already know; connect with them on LinkedIn or via email? What can you share with them in exchange? Use the following table to help.

Who	Why	What	How	And
Do you want to meet?	Do you want to meet them?	Is the one thing you want to know?	Are you going to reach out?	What is the value exchange / follow up?

3. Expand your network

The next step is to look at the key people you need in your network. There's a network assessment tool to help you do that in detail.

Visit www.janinegarner.com.au/network to determine how good your personal network is right now and to identify the gaps.

Facet 9

Collaborate

My brother and I used to love playing Atari games as kids. We were never lucky enough to have an Atari of our own but would hang out for the days we could head to our cousins' place to play Pac-Man. Even better were the evenings when our parents would take us to the local club where we were given a few 20-pence coins to play on the Atari arcade machine and bags of scampi fries (a savoury mainstay of the British pub) to entertain ourselves while they caught up with friends. I'm sure if you're a 1970s or 1980s kid you'll have some other such fond memory!

Back then, Atari was the bee's knees, a pioneer of the arcade video game and home computer market. You could say it was the 'Apple' of the gaming world, a multimillion-dollar industry that, during its golden years, sold over 30 million consoles and hundreds of millions of games.

That was until competition intensified and a Japanese brand, Nintendo, entered the market with a big vision to expand across the globe. They originally approached Atari to work together. Negotiations began. They even got as far as drawing up final contract papers but at the very last minute Atari pulled the plug after seeing one of its main competitors demonstrating a prototype of Nintendo's game, Donkey Kong. Atari took this as a sign that Nintendo were dealing with their competitor too.

Although the issue was cleared up a month later, by then the market had changed considerably. Cheaper copycat gaming products were everywhere, the market became saturated and in 1983 the video-game crash hit. According to reports that year, Atari produced 12 million cartridges and only sold 5 million. Ted Trautman wrote in *The New Yorker* that the 'demand for video games had fallen so much that the company dumped fourteen trucks' worth of merchandise in a New Mexico landfill and poured cement over the forsaken games to prevent local children from salvaging them'.

Meanwhile, Nintendo predicted what was coming and developed a lockout technology system that prevented any unlicensed software from running on its consoles. Nintendo grew from strength to strength. The iconic Super Mario brand went on to sell over half a billion games and is still the best-selling video-game franchise in the world, according to Guinness World Records.

Atari's financial problems, on the other hand, worsened and the company finally collapsed. Nintendo's president Hiroshi Yamauchi said, 'Atari collapsed because they gave too much freedom to third-party developers and the market was swamped with rubbish games'.

The problem was that when little unknown Nintendo went to big brother to ask if they could play together, Atari said no out of fear of competition and a lack of honesty and trust.

But imagine what would have happened if the two had joined forces? Maybe Atari would not just be around today but would be a world leader.

In this fast-moving world, where we all have to make decisions quickly, move faster and continue to chase those clients and those sales to lock down business to secure revenue and our security, so many of us are at risk of becoming Atari.

In our speed to get things done we risk:

- being stuck in our old ways

- believing we know everything and already know the answers

- keeping our eyes blinkered to opportunities to work together and instead stay siloed in our thinking.

Collaboration is a critical skill needed right now and it is critical for the future.

Work together or die alone

Deloitte's recent future of work research stated that 65 per cent of the C-level executives surveyed have a strategic objective to transform their organisation's culture, with a focus on connectivity, communication and collaboration. In addition, a new study by Steelcase found 90 per cent of people say collaboration is essential to creating new solutions and ideas.

Over the past couple of decades, we've seen the drive for increased collaboration across all sizes, shapes and types of businesses and teams. As a result, all of us have been significantly impacted by the amount of time we're having to spend in team-based work versus solo work.

There's no question that collaboration has moved from a 'nice to have' ideal to the 'must have' strategy that leaders around the world are addressing. No matter where you sit in your company or the size of your business, we're all challenged with increased competition and a need to continue to be relevant and in demand. We're all active participants in a race to understand what our clients and customers need and then deliver something more innovative, more fantastic, more life-changing than someone else.

In recent years, collaboration has been pushed down our throats 24/7 from the playground to work: 'C'mon let's all get along and work together'. Collaboration even made *The Lego Movie* theme tune: 'Everything is awesome, everything is cool when you're part of a team.'

It's featured on mission statements and within company values as we build 'one company, one team'. Brands and people are 'collaborating' to create something new and different. I even wrote a book about it: *From Me to We*.

Collaboration is definitely one of the ongoing business buzzwords. It:

- is the most indispensable tool of an organisation

- has become the fuel for continued business efficiency in everyday tasks

- is the essential key to improving the outcome of every business's activities.

So how come it's often so much harder to collaborate than it sounds?

There's no doubt that when talented, highly motivated individuals with their diverse ideas, experiences and opinions work together on a shared objective, great things can be achieved. By working together, we can build upon one another's strengths — we can minimise one another's weaknesses and imperfections to create robust, highly productive and cohesive teams that can move quickly together.

But true collaboration is more than bringing a team of people together to brainstorm ideas. It's more than a collation of sticky-note ideas on a wall or motivating words on branded coffee cups. It's more than joining forces to get something done and it's certainly more than simply sharing resources and opportunities.

For collaboration to work like a well-oiled machine it requires everyone to be connected on the same goal, whatever that may be: developing a go-to market strategy for a new product, running an event, developing an innovative training program, recruiting a new team, writing a book or creating a social media campaign. Every project requires everyone involved to bring their brilliant selves to the project being done. It requires the removal of all bullshit and pretence. If self-doubt enters the system, if comparison-itis, blame, denial, imposter syndrome, worries about imperfection and showing our weaknesses become elements that we hide behind rather than push through, then all we're doing is faking it till we make it and the opportunity that exists within the potential collaborative work will never happen. It will ultimately create tension within ourselves and among the people we're working with.

Collaboration is fundamentally hard because it needs everyone involved to be brilliant, too.

What does success look like?

During my interview with Stephen Scheeler, former CEO of Facebook Australia and New Zealand, we discussed the importance of asking more curious questions to develop a better understanding of the problem and so enable the development of better solutions. Stephen shared a story about some work he was doing with the leadership team of an airline. The leadership team was asking him what Facebook, Amazon or Google would do if they were running the airline. Stephen started asking them deeper, more curious questions in the pursuit of trying to understand the real friction for the airline's customers and he asked, 'How much do you know about how well people sleep on your plane? Sleep is probably the biggest friction that there is in long-haul travel. Sleep is terrible, we all know; we have all experienced it'.

The team responded with answers around managing the spiciness of the food, watching alcohol intake and heating levels and naturally shared the nice luxurious designs of flat beds in first class to support a better quality of sleep.

Stephen challenged the executives again suggesting that they didn't really understand the quality of sleep between row 3C and 30C. 'You've put no insight into the huge customer friction that exists.'

Stephen argues it's not good enough that we don't know the answers to these more difficult questions. He asks how we can possibly explore the right solutions if we don't know what we're trying to solve. By way of example, Stephen shares what a true customer experience organisation would do: 'They would find sensors, for example, and embed them in the cabin of the plane. Sensors so good that they can understand through monitoring the atmosphere how well people are sleeping in the seat just below the sensor. And if those sensors didn't exist those companies would go out and they would invent them. They would hire smart people and invent the technology to help them find the answers.'

Stephen's example provides some key learnings for all of us when we're deciding whether to collaborate or not. Too many of us risk entering into a collaborative workspace, project or opportunity without actually asking ourselves the exploratory questions of:

1. What problem are we really trying to solve here by working together?

2. What does success actually look like?

Asking these questions is about disrupting the present situation and getting curious about a new future. It's about thinking about the road less travelled and going deeper to uncover the root problem.

The risk of not getting clear is that we follow the shiny stuff; get caught up in other people's ideas and direction and taken out of our own lane; risk achieving others' objectives but not necessarily our own; and get caught up in the excitement of 'hey, let's do something together'.

Getting clear on why you want to collaborate in the first place, what problems you can solve together for mutual success and what the measure of ultimate success is, are critical to the foundations of collaboration.

We need to absolutely continue to explore opportunities to do more and to do better. But we equally have to remember that collaboration is always a choice.

Working together has to be right strategically and energetically. It's your choice to invest time and energy in working together knowing that together there's a better outcome. It has to be right for the bigger picture and vision. Due to our individual limitations on time, resources and energy, by choosing to collaborate, we'll always be giving up on investing the time, energy and quite possibly money on something else.

Success can be measured in so many ways: a breakthrough in thinking, a lift in sales, a new product offering, happiness and fulfilment, a merging of teams or businesses, improved productivity and enjoyment, and learning about what to do next time.

In fact, you only have to look at the latest music chart to see a rock star teaming up with a rap star. But for every Eminem and Dr Dre, there's a Justin Bieber and Busta Rhymes.

Unfortunately, too many of us jump straight into the project without discussing and agreeing on the boundaries and parameters of the task at hand and then, like a rocket trying to get to the moon with no map, we collectively spin, zig-zag or go round and round in circles, getting increasingly frustrated at not getting any closer to our goal.

Taking a moment to get clear on why you're collaborating, the problems you're collectively trying to solve and what success looks like is critical to ensure you're fully in or fully out.

The next time you get an opportunity to collaborate, ask:

1. What problem are we really trying to solve here by working together?

2. What does success actually look like?

The sum of the parts

During my time at Harvard, Professor Ron Heifetz encouraged us to imagine our work as a pepperoni pizza and the people involved in the work as slices of the pizza. He added that much like each slice of pizza has different bits of the ingredients and is never quite the same, the people involved in helping us achieve our work are different too.

Collaborative work is much like a pepperoni pizza. It's made up of multiple stakeholders, each bringing their uniqueness — their perspectives, loyalties and values — to the table. Heifetz shared with us that every single person involved in the project has something to lose. And every individual is driven by their own primary need — the need to be the smartest in the room (ego), the need to be liked (intimacy) or the need for agency and control (power).

Everyone is unique. Take time to understand their differences so you can nurture an environment of successful collaboration, value exchange and sharing of ideas.

In 1943, the US Army's Tactical Air Command (TAC) met with Lockheed Corporation to express its need for a jet fighter to counter a rapidly growing German jet threat. One month later, a young engineer by the name of Clarence L 'Kelly' Johnson and his team of young engineers hand-delivered a proposal for the XP-80 Shooting Star jet fighter to the TAC. On a handshake, with no contract but with a very definitive success measure, the go-ahead was given for Lockheed to start development on the United States's first jet fighter effort. Four months later Kelly Johnson and his team designed and built the XP-80 in only 143 days.

Because the war effort was in full swing there was no space available at the Lockheed facility for Johnson's project. Consequently, Johnson's collaborative team operated out of a rented circus tent next to a manufacturing plant. Each member of Johnson's team was cautioned that design and production of the new XP-80 must be carried out in strict secrecy. No-one was to discuss the project outside the small organisation, and team members were even warned to be careful how they answered the phones.

This is a wonderful example of so many things related to collaboration but none more so than the clear appreciation for the right people with the right inputs to support the ultimate goal of delivering the XP-80 on time. As Kelly Johnson said, 'We are defined not by the technologies we create, but the process in which we create them'.

Clarity around who really needs to be involved to drive momentum, and why, builds mutual respect and understanding. I mean, seriously, how many times have you been invited to a 'collaborative project' and every person and their dog seems to have come along too. Or what about that collaborative project you were forced to be on where there's always that one person who doesn't equally pull their weight but seems to ride shotgun towards the required destination with little effort or energy?

Get clear on who needs to be involved and the expectations around inputs.

Ask yourself:

- Who needs to be involved?

- What experience are they bringing to the work?

- What are they expected to contribute?

- Do they bring an alternative, different and potentially challenging perspective?

A collision opportunistic environment

In the book *Forever Skills*, authors Kieran Flanagan and Dan Gregory write,

We create artificial partitions and barriers between information, between roles and responsibilities, and create departments of expertise that actually reduce our capacity to communicate internally and diminish the chances of 'happy collisions' of ideas.

Daniel Coyle adds to this thinking about creating the right environment for collaboration in his book *The Culture Code*. He states, 'Collisions ... are the lifeblood of any organisation, the key driver of creativity, community, and cohesion'.

For collaboration to work, and to work well, we need to facilitate a safe environment.

Kieran, Dan and Daniel are suggesting that for collaboration to work we need to create environments that enable just the right amount of tension for ideas, debate and discussion to bubble to the surface. An environment where people feel safe to voice their opinions, share their feelings, disagree and freely exchange thinking without any fear of judgement;

ultimately an environment where people feel safe enough to bring their own individual brilliance into the room and know that by coming together, as Aristotle said, 'the sum of the parts is greater than the whole'.

Too many organisations today continue to operate amid an underbelly of fear. Headcounts are suddenly chopped, budgets are slashed, people leave with no notice and aren't replaced, career conversations don't happen and numbers become the ultimate measure of success. Why?

Leaders are caught between two worlds: one that thrives on volatility and one that craves stability. The ongoing tug of war that ensues between the pursuit of growth and innovation on one side and a desire for control and consistency on the other is challenging traditional business structures to become more fluid and blended. Innovation and invention are now necessary tools for success, and agility and decisiveness prerequisites for speed to market.

If silos exist, collaboration will never happen. A silo mentality is a major barrier to innovation, profitability and achieving results. It's one where:

- departments, divisions, sectors and individuals don't share information with others

- power struggles drive a lack of cohesion and cooperation

- productivity and efficiency are challenged as resources are misallocated because departments and individuals protect their own backyard

- inconsistent messages are shared among the people involved

- someone's ego may be more important than the team, the project or the goal, and things break down quickly.

I recently heard a fabulous analogy for a safe environment. Think of it like you're cooking a stew. If the heat is too low, it will take forever for the vegetables to cook. In the same way, it will take forever for ideas to bubble to the surface as people instead sit watching, listening and observing, keeping quiet because they're unsure of the rules. Turn the heat up to uber high and the vegetables cook way too quickly. In much the same way if there's too much heat, fear or anxiety in a room, people will either enter into fight-or-flight mode, going on the defensive and attacking or shutting down and keeping quiet out of fear. The challenge is to get the cooking temperature of the environment just right, so that everything is marinating beautifully, to create the yummiest, tastiest meal.

Author Simon Sinek said in his TED Talk *Why Good Leaders Make You Feel Safe*, 'If you get the environment right every single one of us has the capacity to do remarkable things'. Sinek says that belief, trust and cooperation are created when people feel safe; and remarkable things happen when leaders make their team feel safe.

What can you do to ensure the temperature is just right within your team to facilitate and encourage the sharing of ideas and opportunities?

Get off the dancefloor and onto the balcony

With any collaborative effort, despite the best intentions and even when the why, what and who have been clearly established, things can get tricky. This is when, as Ron Heifetz also shared with us during my time at Harvard, we need to get off the dancefloor and onto the balcony as a way of maintaining perspective.

Ron shared that when we're on the dancefloor we're among everything: in the detail, moving and behaving based on the collective energy of the room. Being on the dancefloor is where forward momentum and growth happens. It's where you can learn because you're in the moment. But when things start to feel odd, or your intuition is telling you that things don't feel quite right, this is when Ron advises that we need to get off the metaphorical dancefloor and step up onto the balcony to maintain perspective and reconnect with the bigger picture.

The balcony is a space where you can identify what you don't understand at that moment in time. It's a space of observation and reflection, of asking:

- What do I need to understand more of?

- What's really going on here?

- What more information do I need to seek?

- What am I noticing about myself?

The balcony is the place where you choose what action is needed next before going back to the dancefloor to learn. The balcony provides an opportunity for self-leadership, to intentionally slow down, reflect and decide your next action.

Ron also discussed the risk of sitting on the sidelines. He shared that this was a place where we're pre-occupied with ourselves. I would add that this is a place where fear, imposter syndrome and doubt kick in and stop us getting involved. This is when you have to go back to Law 1 and get out of your own way, choosing instead to own your spotlight and step into the brilliant version of you.

A real-life example of this is an exercise I run during my collaboration workshops.

Essentially, the room is split into groups. Each group is given a different set of resources and the brief is to work collaboratively to build the tallest free-standing tower they can with the resources available. Almost immediately the individual groups go into competition, despite having spent a whole day in workshopping collaboration, I might add! They huddle together and get to it, experimenting with various ideas of engineering mastery to build a tower from tape, lollipop sticks and straws.

During the exercise most people stay on the dancefloor, moving with the energy of their team and the room. Occasionally I observe the odd individual stepping onto the proverbial balcony, taking a look around, noticing that different groups have different resources. Some may even quietly voice 'let's collaborate'. I can see the cogs in their head turning, but few take action.

It's only during the debrief, when we all get onto the balcony and explore the perspective of what went on, that we're able to see:

- the immediate human need to compete

- that they had not listened deeply to the brief or even each other at times

- that they had not asked questions to clarify understanding

- that they had not created a safe space where others could share their thoughts.

FYI: In all the years of running this exercise only one group has ever worked collaboratively to create the tallest tower they could together!

The next time you have an issue to solve in your business, try getting off the dancefloor and looking at it from the perspective of the balcony. You might be surprised by what you see.

Share the love

I recently spent a morning with four other business leaders 'Cooking for a Cause' with OzHarvest, an Australian food rescue charity founded by social entrepreneur and Order of Australia recipient, Ronni Kahn in 2004.

Donning bright yellow aprons and under the expert guidance of chef Fiona (thank goodness for this as I'm no whizz in the kitchen!) we got on with the business of cooking up a storm: chicken curry and spicy potato patties using rescued food. Our success measure was very clear: cook as many meals as we possibly could, in two hours, to feed as many homeless people as possible.

This success measure was doubly important after watching a video highlighting the friction that exists in Australia:

- four million Australians have 'food insecurity'. That is, they don't know where their next meal is coming from!

- one million of these are children.

And to top it all off, the statistics are getting worse — not better (I have no doubt readers in other parts of the world will be equally shocked at the levels of food insecurity in their own countries).

After hearing these very real statistics, speaking to volunteers and hearing stories firsthand, our measure of success was absolutely front and centre: we were determined to work together to maximise success by cooking as many meals as we could.

Together, over two hours, we chopped and peeled and stirred. Together, we cooked, we tasted, we put our energy, hearts and our souls into all we were doing. Together, we listened to stories, were inspired by greatness, shed tears at the unfairness of the world — and before we knew it, our time was up. We had prepared really good food with love, and enough to feed 100 people. Wow!

Yet the collaborative effort of OzHarvest is way bigger than the five of us that day were. With over 2000 volunteers and 160 paid staff, OzHarvest rescued 21 million meals on a budget of close to $15 million in 2018. The vision Ronni had that started OzHarvest could not have eventuated if people hadn't been working together towards the same goal. Every volunteer knows exactly what they're expected to do during each shift to hit the numbers. They're all working towards a purpose and a goal.

This is the power of collaborative effort!

What do you need to change today to better collaborate into tomorrow?

Brilliance in action

1. Define success

Thinking about a collaborative project in your business or area of responsibility. What does success look like? What are the measures of success for you?

2. Get curious

Take a moment to think about a collaborative success that you've experienced at work. Was there anything about the project/work environment that supported its success? Think about the people involved. What types of behaviours were evident?

Now think about the opposite, an example of when things didn't go so well, and get curious about why. What was the environment like? What types of behaviours were at play? Were the right people involved in the project? Was there a unified goal?

3. Create a behaviour manifesto

Create a standard operating document or manifesto of your shared expectations around working together. What are the key expectations and acceptable behaviours? Include 10 key behaviours that everyone involved will commit to, and hold each other accountable.

Watch out!

Now that we know what we have to work towards when it comes to Law 3 and connecting with intent, we also need to be aware that there are forces working against us achieving mastery of this law.

The three shadows to watch out for are:

1. Dream stealers

2. Judgement

3. Loneliness.

Let's explore each now.

1. Dream stealers

I once had a boss who was a great connection, on paper — female, successful, results oriented, a great supporter of me and my work. Over time, however, as my success and network of influence grew, her behaviour changed.

Once-productive meetings became discussions of negative details; my big ideas, which had once been embraced enthusiastically, were shut down; my personal ambitions were devalued and marginalised.

I was clearly and continually put back in my box. A woman who had once inspired me had now begun to limit me.

Dream stealers are the antithesis of change and momentum, of networking to mutual benefit, of keeping you on your unique path and helping you move towards your personal dream of success. And they're everywhere — at the water filter, in the office canteen, sitting next to you, even at home — so beware.

They're friends, colleagues — even family members. And while some of these dream stealers genuinely want to protect you and really do think they have your best intentions at heart, they'll subtly put doubt in your mind. They'll erode your confidence in your own abilities.

Dream stealers are the sappers of positivity. The drainers. The ones who don't add constructive thoughts to your vision and dreams for you. They may not understand the journey you're on — and while that's okay, instead of providing support and encouragement to 'go for it because I know you can do it' their commentary keeps you small and feeds the self-doubt. It activates that really annoying, niggly inside voice to convince you 'you can't', 'it won't work', 'it isn't safe' ... repeat, repeat, repeat.

This means:

- you stay where you are
- you stay small
- your dreams are squashed.

But you can put a stop to this incessant noise that drowns out dreams, thoughts and belief. Take ownership and control of the key people in your personal circle of influence — at the end of the day it's up to you to choose.

Become aware of the impact commentary is having on you and curious about the intent. If it feeds self-doubt, eats away at your confidence, encourages resistance and keeps you small then the Dream Stealers are in action and it's up to you to walk away.

I make no apologies for the fact I choose who I let into my personal network. They're people who add to my energy, not who deplete it. We forget that we all have a choice. We can choose not to hang out with negative people who drain us or squash our dreams. We can choose not to spend time with people who frustrate us.

Don't worry about the people who are passengers in your life, the ones who take, take, take and when something better comes along, they hop right off your bus and onto someone else's (we all know them!). Focus instead on the people who matter, the really meaningful relationships.

We get to choose to create and design the life we want and the people in it, so:

- choose to play their game by their rules *or* play your own game in the way you want

- choose to live the life others want for you *or* live the life you want

- choose to take on others' emotions, fears and insecurities *or* take control of your own energy, mindset and momentum

- choose to listen and believe their story *or* choose to walk away and ignore them.

Have the courage to walk away and instead find those people who will not only dream with you but will offer input, thought and insight to ensure you're moving in the direction of your goals.

2. Judgement

What you think and believe is only what *you* think and believe. It's not necessarily true or right. It's not representative of everyone. It's quite simply your view and your view only.

And yet often we overlay our own belief system, views and opinions on others. We judge others and this stops us engaging the right way. Our judgement gets in the way of engagement. It stops curiosity because we think we already have the answers. Some of you may be reading this and saying to yourself, 'Yeah, I've heard this before. I get it, but it doesn't work. She doesn't understand my life'. Why have you read this far into the book then? (See, I just judged you without meaning to.)

Let's just admit it once and for all that judgement, unconscious bias — whatever you want to call it — exists in *all* of us. We choose to see what we want to see and with that we judge. We judge the working parent, the non-working parent, those with children, those who choose not to have children, the single parent, the divorced parent, the straight couple, the gay couple... We judge those gracing the front covers of our magazines while standing in line to pay for groceries: 'Of course they look amazing; they have so much help, money, fame (insert specific judgement).' We read trash and watch reality television because we want to know the ins and outs of others' lives so we can judge.

What chance of engaging in the right way have we honestly got if we're constantly judging each other's lives and career choices rather than embracing what individuals are doing and standing for?

Start noticing what's going on for you. When you're judging, simply try to give yourself a virtual telling off and get with the moment. Get curious and instead ask:

♦ What's really going on for the other person?

♦ Who are they loyal to?

♦ What do they value?

♦ What could their perspective be?

And most of all, ask yourself what do they have to lose in the situation?

I was recently chatting to Karl, who had moved from a long tenured career in one large, global multinational to a new, more senior position in another, smaller, relatively new player in the same industry. The new company had evolved from start-up to a successful, competitive player and many of the management team had been there since inception. Karl started sharing with me his frustration at the managing director and some of the leadership team around a lack of speed, decision making and processes that he believed were needed to facilitate the next stage of growth and culture evolution. I suggested he get curious about each of his new colleagues and explore for each their perspective on what was happening in the business, what they valued most about their roles, the company and the people, and most importantly I asked Karl to think about what each person had to lose. He stepped off the dancefloor and onto the balcony (like we discussed in Facet 9) and this allowed Karl to widen his perspective, slow down his thinking, and develop more understanding and more appropriate strategic next steps.

We all have something to lose: face, ego, social proof, status, our job, revenue, clients, money, time, what we thought was true.

To engage in the right way and to build connections that matter we need to watch out for judgement and always be curious about what could really be going on for ourselves and others.

3. Loneliness

In a 2018 article published by the World Economic Forum titled 'Loneliness is a much more modern phenomenon than you might think', author Amelia S Worsley explains that in the 17th century people who were lonely were mostly away from the city and overcoming this simply meant returning to 'society'. However, she maintains, now loneliness is more difficult to overcome because it has moved 'inward' — it's now in our minds so even being with other people or in a city environment can't solve it.

Worsley adds, 'Modern loneliness isn't just about being physically removed from other people. Instead, it's an emotional state of feeling apart from others — without necessarily being so'.

Many of us, despite spending days surrounded by people, having things to do and lots of activity around us, surprisingly will at some point voice a feeling of loneliness. A lack of support, a sounding board to debate and discuss, a feeling that everything rests on our shoulders and a sense that there's no-one there for us often fuel these feelings of isolation.

But are you really on your own or is it more about the choices you're making? Are you perhaps choosing to not reach out, to not connect, to not ask for help, to not trust those who care about you and your success?

It's time for all of us, as individuals, to think about how much quality time we're really gifting the key people in our network. Good, quality time to chat openly, to explore, to debate, to ideate, to simply hang and enjoy each other's company. It's time for all of us to become more aware and more present with what's truly going on for those around us — those we care about, who inspire us, whom we respect, whom we also trust — to ask, 'How are you today? Is there anything I can help you with? Let's catch up!'

Your key network is there for you and closer than you think — just ask.

Law 4: Be Heard

Magnify your influence

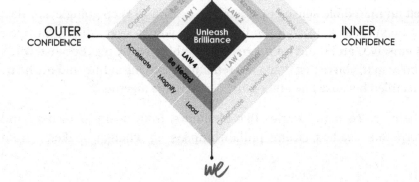

Be the best you, the most successful you.
Be influential, be visible and become professionally famous in all that
you want to do.
Magnify others always to become their brilliant selves too.

After experiencing the personal heartbreak of birthing three premature babies, Melinda Cruz established the Miracle Babies Foundation in 2005 with the help of Liverpool Hospital's Newborn Intensive Care Unit (NICU) and a group of mothers, who all bonded through their NICU experiences. They shared the same common desire of wanting to support other families of miracle babies and give back to the wonderful hospitals that care for them.

Melinda says, 'I didn't set out to change the world. I gathered some papers and went to the head of the unit where my boys were born and just thought I'd start a local group ... and then it exploded'. Not only has Melinda built a foundation that has a long-lasting legacy, she's been inducted into the 2013 Australian Businesswomen's Hall of Fame, and was awarded the title of Honorary Research Associate by the University of Sydney. She now travels the world providing insights and support to change the world of medical assistance for premature and sick newborns.

The impact that Melinda continues to make is extraordinary. When I asked her about this she shared a wonderful story of a doctor who approached her a couple of years ago at a conference in Italy saying, 'Every year thousands of babies are born, that's thousands of parents that are impacted and I've waited my whole career for someone like you'.

She added, 'I remember being quite overwhelmed, but at the same time felt an incredible sense of pride and a reason to keep going every day. You don't realise that all the little things you do every day, layer upon themselves and build up to create something really big. Because when you're in it, you're just doing it. I remember looking at him and my heart just filled because I just thought, "We're in this together"'.

There are so many stories like Melinda's, from business owners and corporate leaders, from philanthropists to change makers, from individuals to groups. What these people have in common is a determination to make a difference and lead change no matter how large or how small; the courage to step into their own spotlight to share their message, to be heard, and with a determination to magnify others around them to do the same.

In reflecting on her journey, Melinda says, 'When you share yourself and your vision and you get other people on board to share that vision too, then you can absolutely make a huge difference. The key is not to be afraid of how big your vision can become'.

As the US poet and writer Marianne Williamson so beautifully put it: 'And as we let our own light shine, we unconsciously give other people permission to do the same. As we are liberated from our own fear, our presence automatically liberates others'.

So where are you right now?

Take a look at this diagram.

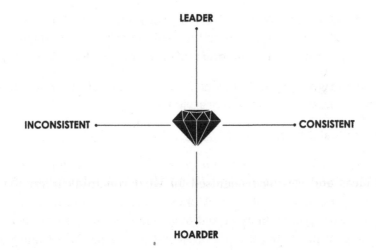

Where would you currently rate yourself in terms of whether you're magnifying your influence and that of others?

- *Hoarder or leader?* Thinking about the impact you're making right now and the influence you're having in your business or industry, where would you place yourself along the vertical axis of hoarder or leader?

  - Do you feel like you're seen as a leader in your business or industry? Are you known for what you know, for what you do and the impact you have on others? Are you ultimately a leader of others and actively sharing your thoughts, providing direction and influencing others?

  - Or are you hoarding your ideas, keeping your thinking to yourself? Are you following and not leading?

- *Inconsistent or consistent?* And where would you place yourself on the horizontal axis of inconsistent to consistent?

  - Are you consistently being asked for your opinion, to speak and to lead? Are your behaviours and how you present yourself within your business and externally to a wider audience consistent? Are you in demand?

  - Or is the way you behave, lead and share your thinking inconsistent and sometimes sporadic? Are you going with the flow of others' thinking and opinions? Are you hiding?

Take a pen right now and draw an 'X' on the diagram to show the spot that best represents where you're at right now.

Done it? What did you notice?

You may feel like you're leading your area of responsibility, sharing your ideas and getting recognised for what you think internally but increasingly frustrated at the lack of exposure to a wider audience. You may see other people being asked to speak, to sit on panels; they may even be posting their thinking on social media platforms and you're looking at them, knowing you really could be doing the same but not sure how. If this is the case, you'll place yourself in the top left-hand quadrant.

Alternatively, you may be feeling pulled in 101 directions, doing a lot of stuff and in demand every which way you turn. But you know you have more to share. You may have ideas, opinions and thoughts running around in your head that you would love to be able to put on paper to share. You may have an innovative idea for your company but don't know how to structure a presentation pitch. You're stuck hoarding your ideas with a desire to become more. If this is the case, you'll find yourself in the bottom left-hand quadrant.

Law 4, Be Heard: Magnify your influence is all about shifting and amplifying your influence consistently so that you lead in your area of expertise and become in demand for what it is you know. Your aim is to sit comfortably in the top right-hand quadrant.

The 3 facets of Law 4

Becoming brilliant and in demand for what you do requires you to be willing to openly share, to stand in your spotlight, to stand up and lead yourself and those around you. This is how we become professionally famous. This is how we shine in our brilliance and allow others to shine too.

Law 4 means you need to practise three facets:

- ◆ Lead
- ◆ Magnify
- ◆ Accelerate.

Let's explore each facet now.

Facet 10

Lead

Cheesy, Ziggy, Benny and Funky George are four of the most incredible teachers on leadership I've ever had the pleasure of learning from (true!). They taught me about the power of trust, authenticity and courage.

I met them during a unique and experiential training session run by Linda McGregor, founder and CEO of Four Legged Sages. Yep — the four teachers are *horses*.

The wonderful thing about horses is that they have no hidden agenda, are masters of emotional intelligence and they have an ability to allow us to see ourselves for what we really are. For example:

- Do we behave in a way that's congruent to what we think?

- Does our body language match what we're saying?

- Are we really building trust with an individual or are we behaving superficially?

Let me explain further.

One of our group that day, Kylie, had to stand in the centre of a round yard while Ziggy the unreined horse ran, bolted and kicked his way around the perimeter. As an observer, watching a 700-kilogram untethered horse run rings around my friend, I could feel her fear and nerves on high alert. Among all of this high and intense energy, Kylie's role was to build trust with Ziggy so that he would choose her to lead him.

It was fascinating to watch the battle between Kylie and Ziggy. Her externally facing, 'I am the leader here', large and in-command gestures with the projected loud, strong voice were obviously incongruent with how Kylie was actually feeling inside. Despite Kylie trying to appear confident to take the leadership position, Ziggy ran and kicked dirt pretty much in her face! He was picking up on Kylie's fear, self-doubt and uncertainty.

All the incongruences between Kylie's external body language and her inner emotions resulted in Ziggy testing, ignoring, challenging and doing the absolute opposite of what was desired. You could almost hear his internal dialogue shouting, 'Why on earth would I follow you when you're scared and uncertain about what you're doing? I don't trust you!'

Kylie had to work hard to get present, to focus, to cut out the external noise and distractions, and to quit listening to the voices in her head. She had to focus on aligning her thoughts with her body language and her desired output: one of building trust, belief and understanding between herself and Ziggy.

She watched intently for connection clues from Ziggy: a slight turning of the ear, the deference of the head drop, a little lick and mouth chew. And she waited, and waited, until the magical moment when Ziggy stopped, turned and calmly walked towards her shoulder, eventually following her around the paddock.

It was incredible to watch!

How many times do we witness leaders saying one thing and behaving in the opposite way? How many times do *we* do the same?

You see, horses behave with you in exactly the way people around you do — it's just that horses are more honest and instant with their feedback than people. They will tell you through their behaviour that they don't believe you, that they don't trust you.

True leadership, the building of trust between people, of creating followership to drive change, takes time and can't be rushed.

And even when it's gained, it can be lost in a nanosecond as a result of incongruence between words and actions.

'Most of us never really think about how leadership "happens",' explained Linda after the session. 'We enter the workplace, we are the boss, or someone is our boss, we try to give direction or follow direction. Sometimes it works and sometimes it breaks down due to a lack of respect, the presence of friction and stress. At worst this leads to a breakdown of positive relationships and eventually work culture. Being chosen as a leader is a different concept, where you need to earn the right to lead, to earn respect and loyalty. To do this you must prove you are worthy to be the leader, that you can be trusted to hold the "reins" of the team and guide them to success safely and fairly. Being a leader means people choose to follow you.'

Leadership is something that's earned and when followership happens, loyalty and longevity are the reward. So, the question is this: 'Are you a leader simply because of your job title or position on an organisational chart or are you a leader because others choose to follow you?'

Make them feel *amazing*!

Michelle Gregory is the co-founder and director of online business Promotion Products, based in Brisbane, Australia. Over the past couple of decades, Michelle and her husband and co-director Douglas have built the business from their humble kitchen table into a multimillion-dollar turnover operation with a team servicing businesses across Australia.

Fourteen years into running the business, Michelle and her husband decided to take a year off with their four children, to live in Spain. They would leave their business in the hands of their employees (yikes!).

At first Michelle thought there would be no way this could happen — seriously, as a business owner, as much as this was a dream, surely it was not a viable option (I can hear your heart pumping now!).

Michelle remembers calling a team meeting one day and saying, 'Right, we're going to live in Spain for a year. We believe in all of you. You know what your job is and you're good at your job. The way our business is set up there is nothing you can do to destroy it that we won't be able to pick up on early. Make the best decisions you know how to make. And if, in looking back, we say maybe we could do that differently in the future, well we'll have that discussion and we'll do things differently in the future. But in the meantime, we believe in you. You got this.'

Michelle and Douglas left for Spain and let the team get on with the work. And the business grew!

On reflection, Michelle shares that the biggest challenge was the belief and trust in her team, believing that they had the ability to achieve something and to do their best work. Michelle says, 'I truly learned what empowering people is all about. It's about saying "I believe you can do this; I believe in your ability. Go do your best and we will evaluate afterwards". I strongly believe that in general people don't get out of bed in the morning and think "Gee how can I stuff up today?" That just doesn't happen'.

Michelle and Douglas's team chose to follow them — they kept the business going, they made decisions that were aligned with the business vision, they felt supported and empowered, they felt trusted and respected, and the results speak for themselves.

Whether you're a one-person practice, a small business owner leading a team, or driving the performance of a larger organisation, it's up to you to make people feel amazing, to bring out the best in them.

As a leader you have the capacity to change someone else's reality about themselves, their work and their environment every day. Leadership is a great responsibility that must not be taken lightly. You have to inspire those around you to perform at their best and to achieve the results they want to achieve. Leadership is connecting, influencing, empowering and equipping others. Leadership is coming from a place of attention out, versus attention in, magnifying the brilliance in others, choosing to listen to understand. Leadership is about creating a safe space that you agitate just enough to unlock ideas and thinking. Leadership is about bringing ideas to life, creating possibility and potential, building security and driving growth. Leadership provides the motivation that drives momentum and change.

Your role as a leader is to:

- make a difference and mobilise change
- create a path for the future, inspiring others to engage with the work that is needed
- meet others where they're at, empowering them to collectively move forward.

As Jim Carrey said: 'The effect you have on others is the most valuable currency there is'.

Are you beige or bubble gum?

Let's be honest, we all know a leader we like but find boring and uninspiring (and if you're struggling, just look on social media or at pretty much any political party).

These leaders:

- find it difficult to compete because their inability to move quickly and make the changes required means new players enter the market, challenge their products or services and deliver solutions that are better, quicker and cheaper
- are secretive and insular, making decisions behind closed doors. They dominate meetings and conversations and miss out on the valuable and colourful debate that happens in hushed voices at the water filter or coffee machines
- lose customers as they move their allegiance to the new kid on the block who's offering a better product with improved functionality or service and a value-add to them, the client

- struggle to attract, recruit and retain talent as staff become disengaged, products become stale, business slows down and profits decline

- are afraid of change, think they know everything and are stuck in their ways, or at worst protect themselves under the guise of process, policy, procedures and 'this is what we do round here'

- churn through the day making small adjustments and readjustments in the hope that these small actions will spark significant momentum in a rapidly changing world — but, of course, it's a mere blip.

What a disaster! I'm sure you'll agree.

So, while I'm a fan of the classic vanilla ice cream with a few sprinkles on top, and maybe some chocolate topping as a treat, when it comes to leadership, the vanilla cookie-cutter approach won't do anymore. You've got to embrace being a little more bubble gum and colourful.

Your teams, the people looking to be led by you, really need you to bring your unique and colourful brilliance to your leadership!

In this ever-changing, uncertain world, we're searching for leaders who have the strength to lead and share, to learn and grow — who are actively curious and willing to give. These leaders are capable of amplifying others; they build a culture that encourages and enables sharing, a culture of commercial collaboration that drives change and innovation. These leaders create the space and freedom to think, debate and ideate. This is a culture in which people from diverse skill bases, demographics, genders and industries have the opportunity to speak and be heard.

Leadership and what we're asking of leaders — of you — has shifted.

To be brilliant, choose to be brave and courageous, to give yourself permission to be you; to embrace your uniqueness and bring all of you to how you lead yourself and others too. Be a leader others choose to follow. Go on, choose to be brilliant, to step up into the leader you want to be, and by doing so, give permission to others to do the same.

This is the only way we're going to change each other, our teams, our organisations and the way we work into the future.

Don't believe this is needed or possible?

I've trained thousands of emerging leaders and top talent, and more often than not I'm asked the question, 'Who can I reach out to for inspiration?' Individuals question why the leaders around them are incongruent, their words and actions misaligned. This feeds a lack of trust, fuels insecurity and creates teams that *do* versus *be*: order takers versus relationship creators. And on the flip side, when people are prepared to unlearn and relearn, to implement the thinking I've shared throughout this book, incredible things happen — teams connect, teams collaborate, teams care.

We all want to be inspired. We want to be engaged. We want to love our work. We want to keep learning and growing. We want to be shown a way, so that together we can drive change.

If you truly want to bring your brilliant leadership self to all you do:

- ◆ be restless, curious and open to opportunity; evolve and try new things; be looking out for 'what's next' at all times

- ◆ be okay about combining your emotional intelligence with economic intelligence and smarts

- ◆ care for the people around you and not just the numbers — you don't want to achieve the number at the detriment of the people around you, surely?

- balance quick thinking and decision-making with a willingness to be flexible and open to change

- be agile, ready, willing and able to keep up with the speed of change

- understand almost perfect is perfect — you don't have to get everything right the first time

- collaborate more and be less mindful of hierarchy and position

- be willing to meet people where they're at, share, mentor others, guide and take a step back

- take an honest and open approach

- create leaders in others and leadership around them

- trust yourself: have a self-belief and inner confidence about the value you're bringing

- share your stories — the ones of success and the ones of failure; let others see you.

This is the leader of the future.
This is *you*!

Let's do a quick check-in now.

1. Are you embracing your wonderfully brilliant, perfectly imperfect self and standing solidly in your spotlight, or are you operating in a way that you think you need to operate as a leader?

2. Are you sharing your vision and dream with all your personal passion and flair, connecting with intent and engaging fully with those around you, or are you hiding, keeping quiet and going through the motions?

3. Are you creating ripples of change and excitement around you that multiply in their impact as people jump on board with your vision, or are you simply making a splash here and there that doesn't seem to amount to anything?

4. Are your behaviours and actions aligned with who you are and who you want to be, or are you presenting a vanilla version of yourself instead of a riot of ideation and colourful innovation?

From below to above

When it comes to magnifying your influence and how to lead, I love the work of Matt Church around leading above the line. In his book *Rise Up: An evolution in leadership*, Matt states that 'leadership is about bringing out greatness in the people around you' and 'making sure the best version of you speaks to the best version of us'.

Matt talks to below the line leadership traits that we need to move away from, such as fear, anger and pride. He encourages us to lead above the line, practising the following three traits as much as possible:

1. courage to let go and grow, taking action in the presence of fear

2. acceptance, replacing judgement with compassion

3. love to teach always and develop greatness in others.

For me, leading from a place of courage is about having the courage to be who we are, to be fully disclosed, vulnerable and real. This requires a level of self-awareness and leading from the inside out. It's about having the courage to be you first and foremost and to be able to connect, as you versus some pretend version of you, with those around you. It's about being clear on your vision for yourself, your value system and your strengths — consistently walking your talk.

Acceptance, for me, is about a deep interest, care and compassion for others. It requires a conscious removal of labels and judgement and replacing this with an intentional curiosity to learn and understand others' perspectives and values. It's also about gaining an understanding of others' possible fears around what they may have to lose.

Leading from a place of courage, acceptance and love is not always easy. Sometimes our days are downright ugly. It can feel like the world and everyone in it is against us and before we know it we're back operating from a place below the line of fear, anger and pride. The opportunity exists, however, for all of us to practise self-awareness and, with focus, choose to take single steps of courage, acceptance and love as frequently as we can. (This is a practice, remember!)

Leading above the line is also about being brave enough to have the tough conversations, to enter into the arena, to discuss, debate and clarify the next steps. It's about understanding when you may be operating from a place of judgement and putting your own interpretation of events into the situation. And teaching always is not simply about the gifting of knowledge and skill. Sometimes the teaching may mean that we have to be brave enough to speak up against unacceptable behaviours or courageous enough to say no to things that are against our own value system or boundaries.

For example, I was recently at lunch with a client who runs an agency. She was angry at clients who were missing project deadlines. She was becoming increasingly frustrated at the impact this was having on her timelines, workload and other client work, let alone the drain on her energy levels as she put in more and more hours to catch up as a result of clients not delivering!

Once the below the line emotions of anger and frustration had dissipated, we started to explore how she could start leading through this situation to above the line. The result? She chose to have compassionate, courageous and difficult conversations with those late-delivering clients, sharing how she fully appreciated life gets in the way, but explaining that missing deadlines comes with consequences and discussing what could be done to minimise the impact for both parties. By having these conversations, she was teaching her clients the importance of prioritisation, following through on commitments and mutual respect. She also realised that by not leading above the line and taking the correct action she was actually doing a disservice to her clients because she wasn't leading the situation or helping them become more; instead, anger and fear were taking over her thinking and decision making. She assessed what she had learned in this process, what her own role and responsibility was. She had to reset her boundaries, and reassess her own leadership behaviours, agreements and contracts to minimise this happening again.

Leading above the line is a choice. It requires us to continually check in on ourselves and those around us. To check and reset. To build the levels of self-awareness, to see what's actually going on. To own our behaviours, actions, intent and how we react and ultimately lead. It requires an everyday focus on practice and effort to lead above the line. And when we're able to operate from this position we can be our brilliant selves and bring the best of ourselves to all we do to help others do the same.

Think about how you're currently operating in a difficult situation. Is it above or below the line? What could you do differently to have a different outcome?

Culture builder or culture killer?

How many times have you sat down, tasked to write your company's mission statement or define its culture?

I can distinctly remember in a former role sitting in a management meeting being challenged to do just this with my colleagues at the time. We initially rose to the request of the definition of the business culture, yet in subsequent discussions, outside of the structured and facilitated day, it became apparent that we had defined our *desired* culture. It wasn't reflective of the culture we actually had!

Culture can't be created through workshops, consultant input, or a printed and framed statement on the reception wall or in the CEO's office.

Culture is something that develops and formulates as a result of the vision, behaviours, actions and values of the entire team — it's the culmination of existing behaviours.

A few years ago, I was engaged by a company that was undergoing a merger and acquisition. The resulting impact on the organisation was a lot of siloed working. It became evident that the team were frustrated at the lack of a positive culture; trust had been eaten away on the back of significant redundancies and internal changes; and there was a lot of talk about poor communication, which was fuelling disengagement throughout the organisation.

I let the whingeing, anger and frustration be shared and then asked, 'Where do you think culture comes from and who can effect it?' Naturally, the immediate answer was the CEO. There's no doubt that culture and behaviour start from the top of an organisation and the leadership team plays a significant part — and I appreciate that, as individuals, sometimes we may be so far from the top echelons of business that we believe we can't impact the change that's needed. However, the reality is that every one of us has the opportunity to effect and create the culture around us. Our own behaviours, and how we're leading ourselves and others, affect the people to the left and right of us, above and below us. The rituals we create, the habits we adopt, the way we engage and communicate — all of these things together feed culture. All of these things have an impact on how other people feel.

This is why it's imperative that we're all clear, as individuals, on our personal value systems. We must live and breathe these values in every behaviour, decision and action we take, trusting our own unique individual leadership style to achieve the best for our own success, our team's success and the financial success of the company.

The soul of the organisation is more than just words.

Your everyday behaviour is what will build or kill your culture.

Nothing to hide, lose or prove

I love these words by retired veteran Ron Harvey: 'Nothing to hide, nothing to lose and nothing to prove.' This is where leaders create the space where people don't have to hide behind titles, positions or something that's fearful. Where they don't have to worry about having something to lose by feeling incompetent and where there's an open environment of learning and debate, of openness to change and difference, where no-one has anything to prove.

When you help people feel safe, trusted and respected, they're able to shape the future of their work and the business because they're engaged and motivated to do great work together.

Isn't that what we all want?

Brilliance in action

1. Follow or flop

Take a moment to write down why people should choose to follow you. Be specific. What is it that you do and how do you want people to feel? Maybe choose five to 10 people in your team and ask them what they think your best leadership traits are and why they enjoy working for you.

2. Lead above the line

Think about a difficult situation you're currently in and how you're behaving. Are you operating below the line from a place of fear, anger or pride? Explore how you could move away from these below the line leadership traits to leading from a place of courage, acceptance or love. What could you do differently?

(continued)

Brilliance in action (*cont'd*)

3. Be beige or bubble gum

Listed below are some vanilla and bubble-gum leadership traits. Circle the ones that you think fit you. What have you noticed? Where could you improve and how?

Beige Traits	Bubblegum Traits
Slow moving	Fast moving
Same network	Diverse network
Stuck in my ways	Open to change
Tell	Ask
Secretive	Inclusive
It's all about the numbers	It's all about the numbers and the people
It's about me	It's about we
Take	Give and take

Facet 11

Magnify

On a school holiday break in Queensland, I was looking forward to hanging out with my family and friends, Andy and Maria. My kids were also excited to see our friends. 'We can't wait for Uncle Andy's cooking' they shouted from the back seat of the car on the way up.

You see, Andy is something of a whizz in the kitchen, always cooking up the best feasts when we visit. On this occasion, he decided to teach the kids how to make their own fresh pasta.

He patiently talked them through the recipe and watched on as they each carefully measured out ingredients. He guided them through the blending and kneading of the dough, explaining the nuances of technique and the importance of letting the dough rest for 'at least six minutes' — and the children sat with their hands protectively covering their own bowl of dough and... they waited (if you've got kids then you'll know what a feat this is).

I then watched on as they took it in turns to roll out their dough, carefully sprinkling flour as required, focused on getting the right length. All the while Andy stood in the background guiding, watching, gently correcting and patiently answering questions. And then the moment of truth as they each fed their dough through the pasta machine, calling on each other to help as they made their own spaghetti.

They cooked it, wolfed it down with lots of commentary about how awesome it tasted, and talked and talked and talked. And all the way back to Sydney they continued to talk, trying to remember the recipe, discussing the benefits of fresh pasta versus packaged pasta and subsequently they researched where to buy a pasta machine.

This experience got me thinking about the opportunity we all have to magnify ourselves through how we lead as well as magnifying the people we work with.

If you think leadership is all about achieving results, managing project plans and developing strategies, then you've got it all wrong.

Leadership is more than getting the job done, hitting that milestone in the project plan or eating the pasta at the end.

Granted the metrics matter, but more importantly it's about how you magnify the people around you and how you share more of yourself to enable others to shine. As Richard S Wellins, senior vice president at management consulting firm DDI, says, 'As a leader your focus changes; your number one priority is to bring out the best in others'.

It's about how we show up and *experience* the work, how it makes us *feel* about ourselves and how we make others feel about themselves.

It's about continuous teaching and mutual learning experiences gained through interacting with others.

It's about a preparedness to push others carefully into their spotlight, encouraging them to give it a go, believing in them and their potential and supporting their success.

It's about leaving a longer-term impression: one that people remember, talk about and share with others, where the experience outlives the moment.

Like Andy, great leaders are able to tune in to the people around them, removing tension or providing guidance as needed. Their supportive presence creates a safe environment to give things a go, to make mistakes, to ask 'stupid' questions. They share unconditionally, teaching always because they know that mastery of anything is an ongoing process that takes time and patience. Great leaders know that creating a memorable learning moment — one that informs and inspires, one that is remembered and that transforms — takes more than a simple telling of instructions.

The effect that you can have through what you do and what you say is one of the most valuable currencies you have. Make sure to invest your currency in the right way.

Value the opportunity you have every single day to magnify yourself and those around you.

Magnify your impact

In 1976, one of my favourite bands ever, the Irish post-punk band U2, was formed. (I realise I'm showing my age.)

Over the years, U2 have played tune after tune, from pubs to stadiums, building their following of fans.

Whether you like U2 or not, it's hard to deny how they use their platform and expertise to incite opinion and debate, to build awareness and to create change. Lead vocalist Bono said, 'As a rock star, I have two instincts, I want to have fun, and I want to change the world. I have a chance to do both'.

U2 delivered one of the most noteworthy performances of the world-recognised Live Aid concert in 1985, and Bono has used his own platform to influence global leaders to write off debt owed by the poorest countries. Through his 'ONE' and '(RED)' campaigns, he enlists organisations and millions of people to combat AIDS, poverty and preventable diseases.

Bono has claimed his lane and willingness to stand for something, to use his position to drive change. Examples of people like this who multiply their impact and make a difference to others are everywhere.

For five years, alongside a group of committed, entrepreneurial women, I ran the First Seeds Fund. Our focus was on giving back at a grassroots level to women and children in neglected communities in urban Australia such as Warwick Farm, just outside of Sydney. Three generations of unemployment, child prostitution and lack of formal education had previously made this a 'forgotten community'; but with the guidance of strong community leaders, and our collective expertise, we were able to make a tangible difference.

One of our projects was the sponsoring of young women and girls in starting their own businesses and selling the resulting products at local markets. We covered every aspect of the business — marketing, business plans, budgeting, design — in order to teach essential skills to girls who otherwise would have absolutely no exposure to any kind of mentoring or futureproofing.

We're in a period of amazing opportunity. One where we can connect and collaborate more than ever before to make a real difference — if we choose to. One where we're absolutely capable of rewriting the rulebook and disrupting the norm — if we choose to. One where if we're authentic and follow our passions, we can build trust, connection and surprise — one to one, more to more, many to many — again, if we choose to.

Walk the talk; own your skills, strengths and goals; and commit to magnifying others so that they can shine too.

Nurture others

Many years ago, I recruited Patrick from the retail shop floor to work as a public relations assistant on one of the fashion brands under my watch. Passionate, determined, hard-working and with a desire to become more, he challenged many company norms. Patrick was the proverbial flamingo in a flock of pigeons — he stood out both in terms of his sense of style and in the way he went about his work.

From day one, I knew he had a passion and talent for more. He had all the elements to build a successful career in public relations and marketing — great relationship building skills, a curiosity to explore, attention to detail, results oriented—he simply needed guidance and active, hands-on sponsorship to nurture and magnify his innate skills and passion and to create opportunities for him to grow and develop. Over four years, Patrick's experience increased, his personal brand elevated and the impact of his work became stronger and stronger.

And over this time, because of this, some of his peers tried to dampen his determination and passion; they wanted him to conform and 'fit in'. They tried to keep him small, maybe out of fear he would be 'better' than them, which is ridiculous, but it happens all the time, right? I supported and nurtured Patrick, his goals and dreams, to keep him shining—and his career subsequently grew and grew. It's an absolute joy to now see him continuing to deliver results, doing what he loves at a more senior level in other organisations. Patrick is truly standing in his spotlight and shining as the unique individual that he is.

Our role as a leader is to develop and unleash the brilliance in others so that they are able to surpass their dreams and become what they want to become.

Magnifying others is energising. I certainly feel that myself. When I see the shift in others; when something I have shared, or an opportunity I have been able to help them with unleashes more; when they're able to stand solidly being their brilliant selves, shining brightly for others to see, achieving what they never thought possible—this is where I truly feel incredible levels of fulfilment and joy. How about you?

Former chairman and CEO of General Electric Jack Welch said, 'Before you are a leader, success is all about growing yourself. When you become a leader, success is all about growing others'.

Conversely, Harvard Business School professor Clay Christensen said, 'The only metrics that will truly matter to my life are the individuals whom I have been able to help, one by one, to become better people'.

I absolutely believe that you'll have even greater influence and impact in your life if you're able to magnify those around you as this creates an immediate ripple effect as they go on to influence others — for years to come.

For example, Megan Larsen is an inspiration to anyone who's not prepared to do things the 'cookie-cutter' way. Her pioneering approach to chemical-free skincare has paid dividends with her brand, Sodashi, stocked in luxury hotels and spas across the world. She shared with me that her driving force in the success of Sodashi has always been people, which is why she's committed to investing in them first. One example is Megan's support and sponsorship of Kim Morrison and the launch of her brand Twenty8 — a range of aromatherapy and skincare products. Megan told me, 'It was evident from the beginning that Kim's energy and enthusiasm for natural skincare echoed my own. Working with others to help them support and develop their businesses is such a joy for me, and in helping others I have learned so much more about myself'.

As Megan has shared in terms of her own development by helping Kim, there's no doubt that your success is a direct correlation to the success of those around you. Anna Beninger, senior research analyst for Catalyst, supports this with her comment, '[You will find] that paying it forward pays back. Developing others really increases your own visibility'.

Take a look around you. What untapped potential can you see? What hidden talent exists in the people closest to you?

What could you do to help them become more?

Two-way talent

Sylvia Ann Hewlett is an economist, the founder of the Center for Talent Innovation and author of the book *The Sponsor Effect*.

In a *Harvard Business Review IdeaCast* in June 2019, Sylvia said,

> [Sponsorship is] *a much more serious thing, because an established leader, ... deliberately invests in a younger talent that they see as outstanding. They open doors for them. ... coach them. ... develop their careers very proactively. ... And in return, they themselves see ... value. It's very much a two-way street.*

Sylvia goes on to share the story of Kate, a senior executive who worked for the tax practice of a professional services firm spotting a young Chinese woman, Shau Zhang, who joined the firm in her twenties. Kate was immediately impressed by the fierce and precise marketing energy that this younger Chinese woman brought to her work but she had extremely poor English. So, Kate persuaded the firm to give her individual, one-on-one English lessons, and she also created some executive coaching to fast-track her presentation skills. Five years later, this was such a success story that she gave Shau the challenge of co-leading with her a new venture at the firm. Shau went on to lead this team and it's now a $100 million-a-year business.

While mentors can counsel an individual, offering guidance and advice based on their own experience, sponsoring and magnifying others is the intentional support of another: taking action, collaborating and sharing what you know and who you know to better someone else. Sylvia Ann Hewlett summed this up perfectly when she said, 'Mentors advise, sponsors act'.

If we're to lead a life of influence, we have to be intentional about magnifying the talent around us. Much like Andy and his pasta-making teaching moment with my children, we have to deliver learning experiences, the chance to grow, and the opportunity to promote and encourage others to become more brilliant.

My friend Ray Pittman says, 'Everybody has potential. I think it is the job of the leader to help their team to find that and to learn how to perform at a higher level both individually and together'.

So, think about:

♦ what specific action you can take that will lift others higher

♦ how you could open doors for others to try new things and practise new skills

- when you could make invaluable introductions that might be a business or career lead

- how to share what you know: your knowledge, insight and advice.

Magnifying others is about securing the present and ensuring that the pipeline of the future generation of leaders, entrepreneurs and philanthropists is solid. It's about ensuring that the future leaders and pioneers have effective role models now, sharing all they have learned along the way and opening the book of their contact base.

Weh Yeoh is the founder of OIC Cambodia, an initiative started in 2013 that aims to establish speech therapy as a profession in Cambodia. He has volunteered with people with disabilities in Vietnam, interned in India, studied Mandarin in Beijing, and milked yaks in Mongolia. Weh shared a story with me that illustrates how magnifying others can begin at any age.

> On my first day at kindergarten I was a young five-year-old, wide eyed and very obedient boy. My teacher, Mrs Pickering, said to me that the boy sitting next to me, Roger, was someone I had to help. She said that Roger couldn't see colours, so I had to help him with his colouring in. She said, 'Anytime he needs a blue pencil you've got to take it out of the little basket for him. Anytime he needs a red pencil, you do the same'. What I learned from that experience was that sometimes all it takes is a little bit of help, to have someone do something for you. That every little bit helps others become better.

Like five-year-old Weh helping his school friend do better, magnifying others is about saying 'I'm willing to teach, to show, to engage'. To break down barriers and sponsor those who you see merit in, irrespective of gender, race, background or old school ties. Take the lead. Step up, step forward and give those who are on their way up the slope the tools to make it to the top of the mountain.

Who needs you in their world to help them magnify their brilliance?

Leave no child behind

Imagine standing up in front of your CEO and senior leadership team, presenting a 10-minute keynote (with no notes or bullet points on slides) on an idea you have for your business — one that's well thought through; that you have been developing outside your day job for the past eight months; that will drive revenue, save costs or create a change in organisational behaviour — with the aim of getting a high five and 'go for it' from your leaders?

Exciting?

Challenging?

Petrifying?

Too right it is. But it happens.

For several years, I've had the honour of working with some of the best and brightest at a global technology firm and every year I'm blown away at the final graduation day as individuals bravely step up and present their innovative idea for the organisation to the CEO and leadership team.

To witness their individual brilliance shining brightly as they step with confidence well and truly into their spotlight is inspiring and it's always fabulous to see their work recognised and thinking reinforced by the leadership team.

At times I have no doubt that these 'students' didn't like me much as I pushed and stretched, challenged and questioned, for the simple reason that I saw so much more in each of them.

But the majority of those at the starting line get to the end of the program, each on their own accord, during a year of change, incredible workload, a significant amount of personal compromise and most of all an inner determination to be their best.

From day one, my team and I commit to the fact that 'no child will be left behind'. We know exactly what's possible if we're able to build trust, and create a safe environment to learn in and the encouragement to do the work. Our commitment is to magnify their inner brilliance, build their confidence and allow them to shine.

When I think about magnifying others I think about what's achieved through this program: helping people move from being scared about sharing an idea, fearful about speaking in public or even nervous about how to put fingers to keyboard to write a well-thought-through white paper, to delivering on all three. It truly is a massive shift for them.

As leaders, to help bring out the best in others, you need to:

◆ create a safe environment for people to try and fail, to question and ask, to explore and be curious without judgement

◆ create a space for personal growth where people are challenged and pushed, encouraged and nurtured as they work towards their own frontiers of competence

◆ respect the individual, acknowledging individual strengths, experience, skills, capabilities and achievements to date and encourage individuals to leverage their uniqueness for themselves and to help others

◆ care about the individual and be truly compassionate about where they're at, their views, personal opinions and inner fears

◆ recognise growth and personal achievements, and acknowledge when new learning has been adopted and personal limitations or barriers are pushed through.

Thinking about your company or team, which of the behaviours above are you strong at and which could you focus on to improve?

How could you make sure you leave no 'child' behind in your team or organisation?

Embrace feedback

John C Maxwell, leadership expert and author, is known to have said to his mentees, 'The good news is I care about you — the bad news is I will be honest'. And it's that honesty that's one of the essentials of magnifying others: the honesty to give true, real feedback.

Feedback is a crucial element to growth and success. Every single one of us needs feedback and support to become better at what we do — we'll only improve if we're willing to hear others point out our weaknesses and opportunities. And as leaders, as individuals, we need to ensure we do this for others.

According to research by Officevibe, an employee engagement firm, 65 per cent of employees want more feedback. So why don't we give more? Because it's amazingly hard to give feedback. We worry about the negative, about hurting someone's feelings. What if they leave my business? What if I upset them to the point where they go downhill rather than up? But as Georgia Murch, author of *Fixing Feedback,* says, 'If we don't invest in our people and give them the feedback they need, we can't expect to have a high performing business'.

Just think about it. Remember a time when you didn't give honest feedback. How did it feel? Did you end up kicking yourself? How many times have you thought 'I wish I had said something at X point', because the result of not giving the feedback at X point ultimately impacted your business and the person you were trying to assist — and not necessarily in a positive way?

I remember at one time debating with myself for a couple of days about how I was going to give constructive feedback and input to someone I respect, admire and who is kicking some serious goals. Round and round in circles I went — should I? Shouldn't I? How do I say what I want to say so that it comes across in the right way? In the end, I approached the conversation from a place of care and compassion. The feedback was well-received, and steps have already been taken (I love working with go-getters!) to make a tricky situation more manageable. From the email I subsequently received, I know that they appreciated what I had to say and the way I said it, even though it was hard for me at the time, and hard for them to hear.

If you approach feedback from a place of care, compassion and wanting to support and guide further evolution and improvement, it will be something that's both well given and well received. If you approach from a place of judgement and attack, telling versus choosing to understand and help, the result is very different.

Liz Wiseman, author of *Rookie Smarts,* believes that magnifying the talent of others is a key component of leadership. She calls leaders who bring out the best in others 'multipliers' who take the time to understand the capabilities of each individual so that they connect employees with the right people and the right opportunities — thereby building a virtuous cycle of attraction, growth and opportunity. That also means giving them honest feedback to help them grow!

One of the subjects of a study by Professors Peter Fuda and Richard Badham, of Australia's Macquarie Graduate School of Management, was Clynton, a managing director of a large German beauty corporation. He had received harsh feedback that he was too direct and that his style was creating dysfunction in the team. Rather than hiding this information from his staff, he chose to be open about his feedback. Clynton bravely discussed his failings and desire to improve at an annual meeting in front of his top 60 managers. The team pledged to help him achieve his goals — and the result? The organisation outperformed its competitors in the six years following the meeting. Wow!

You owe it to others to provide feedback, to avoid any complaints or 'if only' moments later on. Help others take control — and in the process, you'll find that it not only lifts their burden but yours as well.

Show that you give a damn because that's the greatest gift of all.

You are infectious

I remember as a 15-year-old girl, jumping on a plane for the first time with my mum and brother and arriving in Australia to visit family. One day we caught the ferry from Manly to Circular Quay. The adults I was with were chatting to a young woman — she must have been about 25 — and I looked on and listened in with awe. She was originally from the UK, lived in Manly and now commuted every day via ferry to work. My eyes must have looked like saucers as I stared at her in awe of what she was now doing, unable to fathom that this way of travelling actually happened — for me, it was all about the local 30-minute bus ride from my house to Leeds city centre. It's funny looking back because 20 years later I now take that ferry ride on a regular basis.

I know I'm not the only one who has experienced such moments — a brief meeting or conversation that lasts a lifetime.

Imagine all those moments that seemed insignificant to you but have impacted someone else for years to come.

In *Psychology Today*, Tim Elmore writes, 'Sociologists tell us the most introverted of people will influence 10 000 others in an average lifetime'. Wow, and that's just for introverts! Imagine the impact all of us can make!

We can use these moments for good or bad, to energise or to destabilise, to create hope and possibility or to shatter dreams. We can choose to inspire, to feed belief and to fuel positivity, and we can relight the fire in the bellies of others — should we choose to.

Every single one of us has the opportunity to exert our influence and leave an impact in ways and at times we least expect to, which is why it's so important to bring our brilliance to every moment.

Brilliance in action

1. Magnify others

Sponsoring others is about securing the present and future pipeline of brilliance in leaders.

♦   Who are you sponsoring right now?

♦   Who could you sponsor?

♦   Are you actively sharing your knowledge and connections, and opening doors for others?

♦   Are you creating opportunities for others to pursue their goals and dreams as well as pursuing your own?

♦   What improvements could you make?

2. Magnify your impact

How can you extend your impact inside and outside of your work? How can you share more of your thinking within your organisation or industry? Where can you use your skills, expertise and passion to help your local community?

Facet 12

Accelerate

It continues to amaze me how many of us personally invest in financial planners to build financial freedom, trainers to create that perfect body, nutritionists for better eating or meditation teachers for more balance, yet we still fail to personally invest in our own leadership capability. Worse still, when individuals do invest in learning (either out of their own pockets or at the expense of their businesses) it's always astounding how many don't put into practice the learnings — they fail to do the required work, they don't even commit to making a 1 per cent change. They put the learning into their bottom drawer, give up or move on, searching for the next learning fix.

It's all lost in a sea of excuses: too hard, no time, where to start, what's the point!

It was organisational psychologist Karl Weick who said that the best advice leaders can give is 'I don't know', because by saying this leaders are challenging themselves and others to think and explore more. Tom Peters calls it 'cultivating "towering competence"'. Essentially, continually learning more, honing your skills and developing yourself and your thinking to the point that you become known for knowing something is the key.

I get that this learning thing is challenging. It forces us out of the comfort zone of knowing what we know, it challenges us to get comfortable with being uncomfortable, it encourages us to explore and get curious about something new and unknown. It forces us to admit, 'Hey, you know what, I don't know how to do this'.

Seth Godin, in his blog 'Tension vs. fear', says,

Tension is the hallmark of a great educational experience. The tension of not quite knowing where we are in the process, not being sure of the curriculum, not having a guarantee that it's about to happen.

He adds that good teachers create tension, which is what 'active learners' look for because that's what pushes them 'over the chasm to the other side'.

Accelerating your skills and knowledge — learning more — is a self-directed desire and a choice.

It's continuous. We must keep on growing after all our formal education is done — maybe in actual fact our real learning starts the day we leave the safety of the formal education system and enter the education that is life.

Simon Sinek says, 'True leaders do not work to do better than anyone else, they work to do better than themselves. And that's what makes them better leaders'. I couldn't agree more.

Leadership and becoming brilliant is a commitment to improving ourselves, magnifying others and teaching always. It's about stepping forward in a committed direction every day. We never stop learning. Instead we're continually practising and evolving, improving our personal practice to better ourselves as the world continues to move and evolve around us.

Where you're at now and what you're capable of tomorrow will depend on what you do now and what you learn today.

Are you intentional in your learning — to become better, to accelerate yourself and your dreams — or are you well and truly sitting in the passenger seat?

You need fuel

Jobs, businesses, industries and how we work are all changing. Knowledge, however, builds like compound interest, and the more you learn the more you'll grow. It's your knowledge and skills that will stay with you for a lifetime. Investing in yourself is the most profitable investment you can make, and it will accelerate your personal and professional success.

Your experience to date is a gift that no-one can ever take away.

Your current successes and failures provide the foundation for what you know today. Overlay continuous investment in you and what you already know, and this will give you your competitive edge and accelerate your growth personally and professionally, regardless of what's happening in the economy or around you.

Warren Buffett, American business magnate, investor and philanthropist, says the best investment you can make is one that 'you can't beat' — that can't be taxed and that even inflation can't take away from you. He is a massive advocate of learning, saying,

> *Ultimately, there's one investment that supersedes all others: Invest in yourself. Nobody can take away what you've got in yourself, and everybody has potential they haven't used yet.*

In the Netflix series *Inside Bill's Brain*, we witness Bill Gates, founder of Microsoft, carrying a tote bag filled with books everywhere he goes. Every week his assistant refreshes the bag, which holds about 15 books. Gates has a voracious reading habit and is 'joyous about learning', according to friends. Every year, Gates disappears on 'think weeks' with his tote bag of new books. During these weeks he sits, reads, thinks and writes.

I think we need to add a time commitment to learning. For example, how many days over the next 12 months do I want to invest in thinking and learning?

Personally, I invest up to 20 per cent of my income a year on personal development and learning. This will include specific courses, event and conference attendance, books and online learning and intentional conversations (yep, I book in specific lunch dates with an agenda of discussion points) and debates. I listen to podcasts and read articles while on the move and have multiple books on the go, from autobiographies to books with a specific subject focus, and I make a point of sitting and reading every single day.

Find smart people and ask them to challenge your thinking. Encourage them to share where they think you're wrong and then ask them how they know what they know. Dig deeper. Be more analytical. Ask questions. Be a beginner.

While time is the scarcest resource of all, your ability to think, learn, explore and be curious is critical — it's your competitive advantage and key differentiator. Being interesting and great to be around is one thing. Remaining interested in all that's going on around you, curious about new thinking and stretching your personal intelligence bank is the fuel.

The biggest investment you can make is in creating time to think and learn. This will accelerate and magnify your influence and allow you to share with others to magnify theirs.

It's your responsibility to be relevant

Adaptability, complexity of challenges and a need to connect with the right people to do the right work is critical in driving change. And if we don't at least try and keep up — if we don't attempt to remain relevant and current — then we, individually, become defunct and tossed out with the 'maybe I'll recycle that later' pile.

We're living in a world of adaptive challenges where the problems are complicated and complex and not always clear, where the solutions are multifaceted and where we may not always have the immediate answers. The challenges we're facing now can't necessarily be resolved by the solutions that worked before — the world is in a very different place socially, economically, technologically and philosophically.

What you know — your perspective on a problem, your ability to play and explore the edges, to think outside the box, to think differently — is critical. Your experience and achievements so far are awesome, and you have to be brave enough to overlay this existing knowledge with a curiosity to keep thinking differently and deeper, and to explore alternatives. You have to be prepared to keep learning, prepared to be proved wrong, prepared to learn again and prepared to try again.

In the 2019 *Forbes* article 'The 10 vital skills you will need for the future of work', Bernard Marr wrote, 'Since the half-life of a skill has dropped from 30 years to an average of 6 years, it's time for all of us to begin acquiring skills that will make us valuable resources in the future workplace'.

The need for more complex cognitive skills was reinforced by the World Economic Forum's 'Future of jobs report 2018' for the then future (2020), where it identified the top five skills needed as:

1. complex problem solving

2. critical thinking

3. creativity

4. people management

5. co-ordinating with others.

Marshall Goldsmith was spot on when he said, 'What got you here won't get you there'.

Your competitive advantage will come down to your continued relevance and most of all your ability to think. Thinking is your competitive advantage as today and tomorrow requires curiosity, creativity and critical thinking and for you to embrace the opportunities of the future.

You have to commit to continually updating your personal toolkit, invest in your thinking, and embrace diversity of opinion and knowledge. It's more imperative than ever to learn at the edge of your comfortable lane.

Stay interested and stay interesting and you'll improve the quality of your work and life; you'll accelerate your unique brilliance.

Learning is a no-brainer

According to CCSO Business and Development, the benefits of continual personal development and learning go way beyond the acquisition of skill or knowledge. Four of the key benefits the report mentions are that:

1. *your brain chemistry changes.* The more we learn and practise a new skill, the denser the white matter in our brain, myelin, becomes, which ultimately helps us learn even more over time — there's that compounding effect again!

2. *your learning speed increases.* When we learn we stimulate neurons in our brain, and the more neural pathways that are formed the faster electrical impulses can travel, meaning that we learn faster over time. This reminds me of the first time I wrote a blog — it took forever! Now, after writing every week for many years, the words flow more easily and the process is much speedier. They say 'practice makes perfect', right?

3. *you make connections between skill areas.* Our prior experience and knowledge helps us relate to new information and build on the skills we already have. Our ability to connect dots and to curiously explore new solutions to existing problems is enhanced when we expand our knowledge and skill base.

4. *you adapt better to change.* The expansion of your knowledge adds a new level of perspective and this in turn makes it easier to adapt to the inevitable changes in life and at work.

Learning accelerates your brain, your performance and your continued relevance — that's a no-brainer!

Teach and be taught

During my interview with Ray Pittman for my podcast, we were chatting about the changing environment and the need to keep learning as the only sustainable competitive advantage we have.

'Whatever I know today is not enough for five years from now. And if I'm complacent and don't continue learning, I'll fail at some point. So, I've always been a learner,' said Ray.

Ray shared with me how in his late forties he decided to do an MBA. He told me, 'I remember walking in and most times they thought I was the professor, and then I'd sit in the class, they'd give me a puzzled look and then realise I was just a student there to learn too'.

Ray's passion for learning illustrates that learning is and should be something that we never stop doing. It reminds me of the words of Richard Branson: 'The day you stop learning is the day you stop living. We should all pick up new skills, ideas, viewpoints and ways of working every day.'

But here's the thing: it's up to you to surround yourself with the right teachers — those individuals who support you, building your mastery and knowledge so that you can become better every single day. They will spark inspiration, instil values, feed curiosity and help you look for answers. This is essential to accelerating your brilliance and success.

In my bestselling book, *It's Who You Know*, I describe three types of teachers to seek out to include in your inner circle of smarts. They are:

1. *the influencer*: someone who has already achieved your dream and is willing to share all they know

2. *the professor*: someone who constantly pushes you to think better, think deeper and think differently

3. *the architect*: someone who is methodical, astute and financially savvy, helping you lay the stepping stones to your goals.

When I think about teachers helping us see an alternate perspective or explore a different solution to a problem, I think about Great Ormond Street Hospital and the curiosity of two of its doctors: Dr Goldman and Dr Elliott.

Great Ormond Street Hospital treats around 100 000 kids per year who suffer from various heart diseases. But in the mid-1990s, this hospital saw a higher rate in mortality than the usual average, particularly in the handover of patients from the surgical unit to the intensive care unit (ICU). With mounting pressure from the UK government, public and media to find a solution to the increasing crisis, consultants and experts were brought in to try and find a solution.

One evening, doctors Goldman and Elliott came home after a particularly gruelling day and sat watching Formula One. They watched as the 'lollipop man' ushered a car to a halt in the pit stop and the crew changed the tyres, replaced damaged parts and cleared air vents at speed and then ushered the car as 'good to go' back onto the track. The doctors observed a comparison to their own work: in the hospital, the patient comes in, is operated on by a group of surgeons and nurses and is then handed over to the ICU.

And so, the leaders of Great Ormond Street Hospital's surgical and intensive care units started working with the Formula One teams. They invited the British driving team, McLaren, to give them insights into pit stop manoeuvres. They got in touch with Ferrari's pit crew, who invited them to take a look at their practice sessions. They even paid a visit to Scuderia Ferrari's headquarters in Maranello, Italy, where they showed Nigel Stepney, the technical director, videos and pictures of the hospital's handover procedures. Instead of being amazed, Nigel was surprised at:

- how messily the operations were being carried out

- the disorder and chaos of lots of conversations being exchanged between the doctors and nurses

- the lack of a 'lollipop person' — a person in charge who had the responsibility of the flow in and out of the ICU.

New systems and protocols were put in place. The anaesthesiologist became the lollipop person—and the result? Before the change, equipment and information errors sat at approximately 30 per cent and afterwards these dropped by 10 per cent. Wow!

Ultimately the right teachers will push and stretch thinking, challenge ideas and encourage action because they know that on the other side of learning mastery, flowing with the art of constant curiosity and wearing a new 'what if' lens, lies opportunity for more growth, more achievement, more success.

One of Warren Buffett's investments in himself came in early adulthood, when he signed up for a Dale Carnegie public speaking course. 'You can't believe what I was like if I had to give a talk,' Buffett recalls in his biography, *The Snowball*. 'I would throw up.'

But he says, the course built his confidence and it changed his life.

So thinking about your personal development needs, who could become your teacher?

Stop hitting snooze

I get it's easy to sometimes slip into a mentality of 'comfortable shoes'. I tend to see this appearing usually after a period of medium- to long-term stability, when things are going well, and the day-to-day workings of our world are moving along without more than the occasional small problem rippling the surface.

While it may feel like you're breathing easy, if you hit that snooze button for too long and choose to rest in the comfort zone of your new business or personal norm you'd better watch out because in this fast-moving world you can rapidly trip over, and be taken over or side-swept before you even have the chance to haul yourself out of that squishy squashy sofa of your existence.

So continually invest in:

- *mindset and confidence* — build resilience, courage and self-belief

- *creativity* — develop creative and curious thinking, learn to think deeper and more broadly

- *knowledge* — build capability, credibility and self-worth

- *health* — remember my good friend Nikki Fogden-Moore has a saying that we 'can't FedEx our bodies back' and she's right: look after yourself so you're energised to do your best work

- *financial management* — build independence and freedom and the subsequent choice this brings

- *relationships* — the more you build a strong support crew of personal and professional friends around you, the more you'll feel fuelled with support and the happier you'll become.

Invest by surrounding yourself with the right teachers who will stretch you and push you, who will accelerate your brilliance.

Finally, remember...

I remember the first month of being in a start-up. I'd left a large organisation, a team, an IT department, a budget and suddenly I was sitting alone at my desk in the bedroom and all I had was a computer, an idea and a dream. After a solid 20-year corporate career suddenly it was like being back at kindergarten. I had to learn *everything* again — this time it wasn't enough to be the marketer. I had to be the founder, leader, accountant, bookkeeper, IT person, cleaner and caterer, usually at different times in a single day. It was exhausting jumping between big-picture thinking and being in the trenches, from thinking and selling to delivering a service. But that's what life is, a juggle and an ever-evolving process that you have to shift and shape.

The practice of brilliance never ends. It's like yoga and meditation, where you're constantly learning, unlearning and relearning. What worked yesterday may not work today. What's working today may not work for you as you move forward, get a new job, launch a new business or get a promotion.

Leading a life of influence is understanding that at every stage of life and change of circumstance we also have to morph and evolve.

Brilliance in action

1. Fuel up

Identify three self-improvement areas that you'd like to work on over the next 12 months. What are these areas and why do they matter to you?

Think about:

♦ mindset and confidence

♦ creativity

♦ knowledge

♦ health

♦ finance

♦ relationships.

Where could you go or who could you reach out to, to improve these areas?

(*continued*)

Brilliance in action (*cont'd*)

2. Build your knowledge bank

List three books you want to read this year. Go out and buy them or download them. No excuses. Get started now.

Write down three TED Talks and three podcasts you want to listen to. You may have them listed somewhere or have heard others speaking about them. Now it's time to take action. Download them and block out some time in your diary. Develop a learning cadence and make knowledge acquisition a habit.

3. Seek out teachers

It's up to you to find the right teachers to help magnify your influence. Who might these be? Who could you think about following or reaching out to?

Watch out!

The challenge of Law 4 is to own the fact that it's up to you to continually step up and lead, to magnify your influence and that of others and to keep accelerating your growth. It's about continually stepping out of your comfort zone. As Jim Rohn, American entrepreneur, author and speaker, said, 'Leadership is the challenge to be something more than average'.

And so, you have to be on the watch for:

◆ treading water

◆ swimming against the tide.

Treading water

The ability to adjust to new conditions has always been part of human existence. But today, more than ever, we're living in extraordinary times of change and challenge.

So, it's easy to operate from a place of survival rather than growth, a place of complacency rather than curiosity. We forget about the customer, fail to engage teams, struggle to attract, recruit and retain talent, and simply churn through the day making small adjustments and readjustments in the hope that these small actions will spark significant momentum in a rapidly changing world — but of course it's a mere blip.

Status quo is the enemy of change, new ideas, innovation and invention.

Sitting comfortably on the comfort zone sofa, accepting the status quo and resisting change results in complacency and the risk of heading in one direction — down a slippery slope to failure.

Boston Consulting Group states that organisations must today shift their business model and leadership skills to become more adaptive: to be better, faster and more economical than their competitors. The

Harvard Business Review supports this sentiment in the article 'The work of leadership' by Ronald A Heifetz and Donald L Laurie: 'It's tough when markets change and your people within the company don't.'

Philosopher Charles Handy talks about the phenomenon of the 'Sigmoid curve'. According to Handy, the best time to start a new 'curve' is before you reach the peak of your existing one. That way, you'll be starting something new when you still have the resources, and the spirit, to take it to new heights. In contrast, most people think of doing something new only when they've reached the bottom of what they're presently involved in.

The speed of transformation that we're currently witnessing in the way business is being done is challenging us all to think differently—to play on the edge, to seek new opportunity, and above all, to develop innovative ways to communicate our differences, share our authenticity, and deliver our products and services in a way that's relevant today, not yesterday.

The high achievers refuse to accept the status quo; they evolve and align opportunity for themselves and their businesses with the opportunities around them—and they do this all the time; they're restless. They'll zig while others zag. They're agile, action-driven and results oriented. They're focused and directional—strong in commitment and decisive in vision.

Stagnation isn't on their agenda because a curiosity about the future, about ways to make the impossible possible, is the only way to drive change. The businesses that keep their eye on the ultimate goal and also remain willing to change their dance as required to get there will be the ones that succeed.

As Thomas Edison said, 'Opportunity is missed by most people because it is dressed in overalls and looks like work'.

Swimming against the tide

In Australia we teach our children surf safety and in particular what to do if they're caught in a rip. A rip is a strong, localised and narrow current of water that moves directly away from the shore. If you're caught in a rip you can very quickly be dragged out to sea. We teach our children to remain calm and not panic, to float or tread water until they can swim out of the rip and only then swim parallel to shore to escape the current. Trying to swim against the rip is exhausting, as no matter how much effort and energy you expel trying to swim to shore, the ocean is far more powerful.

As we teach our children to remain calm in the face of change, I think the same applies to Law 4. Given the speed of change around us, we can either choose to remain calm and evolve with the changing tide, curious about what we have to do to magnify our influence, or we can swim against it, sticking our heels in the ground, believing we know all we need to know and pushing back against the changes that are happening. Choosing the latter pushes us back into exhaustion land and ultimately affects where we're positioned in Laws 1 and 2.

We're all more successful when all people, departments and leaders are working together through change. Those able to take a step back to establish perspective and effectively communicate often create the strongest tides within their business.

I recently met an incredible force of nature in Jade Hameister, an 18-year-old Melbourne student. In January 2018, at the age of 14, Jade became the youngest person in history to pull off the 'polar hat-trick', skiing to the North Pole, the South Pole, and crossing the second largest polar ice cap on the planet — Greenland. We're talking more than 1300 kilometres over three expeditions in 75 days!

Her story of courage, enthusiasm and inner fire got me thinking about what it means when we don't take chances. What happens when we stay on our personal squishy squashy comfort-zone sofas?

What does getting stuck mean to you? Does it mean that you're stable and able to cope with day-to-day life without feeling overwhelmed? Has it become more about keeping your head down and hidden while all around you goes crazy? Maybe it's about keeping silent with your ideas or opinions, out of fear of shaking things up or upsetting others. Maybe the thought of sticking your neck out, doing something different and possibly failing or even looking stupid is way too scary?

What it absolutely does mean is staying static, not changing, not growing, and in this world of busyness where business is trying desperately to keep up, those sitting in the comfort zone are at risk of becoming irrelevant.

Imagine if the late Steve Jobs hadn't gone back to Apple as its CEO or invested in Pixar. If he'd been happy to say, 'Well, I tried — and it didn't work, so I'll just stay where I think I may be comfortable'. No Mac. No iPhone. No iPad. No visionary steering Apple to extraordinary heights.

There's no denying that stepping out of the safety of where you're most comfortable is scary as hell. It often means big ups and downs — a rollercoaster rather than a gentle turn on the merry-go-round. You'll probably feel as though you're without a safety net much of the time, and that can be extremely confronting. This is when you have to pull on your courage and bravery, tap into the learnings within Laws 1 and 2 and connect with those around you more than ever.

In business, and in life, there's no free ride. It's those people who are willing to challenge themselves, who make themselves accountable for their own success, and ultimately their own happiness, who engage with others — who recognise the need to reach that little bit further or higher — who will end up with the biggest satisfaction.

Of course, we all stumble a little, admittedly — but ultimately?

Swimming with the tide, evolving and changing direction and unlearning and relearning will allow you to continue to excel.

Time to shine

Why did you pick up this book? Be honest now.

Do you want more from life?

Do you believe you can do more with your life?

I believe you can. I reckon you're absolutely brilliant.

In that amazing body and mind of yours exists your inner brilliance. In your teams exist the ideas and innovations you're searching for to drive the change that's needed. And in your business lies the brilliance that will set you apart from the competition, that will give you the edge, that will guarantee your next growth plan.

You have all you need.

All your experiences up to now, all the highs and lows, all the wins and losses, all the high fives shared and failures faced — some of which I have no doubt you'd love to forget — all of it, yep, all of it, has got you to here.

So, it's up to you to decide what's next.

I've worked with so many people just like you — senior executives, business leaders, small business owners, men and women, young and old — and every single one of them has their own stuff going on, their own fears and self-doubts, their concerns about what they don't have and their dreams of what they wish they did have.

We all do.

But here's the thing.

Brilliance does not magically appear — it requires constant work.

It needs us all to slow down, to think, to zoom out, to look in on ourselves. It requires courage and bravery. It requires truth and authenticity.

But really — in this new world we're all learning to live in — what choice do we really have but to become the best version of ourselves that we can become?

If we can own who we are, if we can get out of our way and bring the best of ourselves to our life and our work, then maybe, just maybe, we'll start feeling back in control and make the impact we want to make and the impact we're all absolutely capable of making.

Only when we embrace our own imperfections and rise above our own limitations, and unleash our own inner brilliance, can we truly create the space for others to do the same.

Brilliance is not the result of one action. It's the practice of many, starting with the Laws and Facets in this book.

The culmination of these many individual, separate, personal efforts over time will collectively allow you to have the impact and influence you want to have in your life, your work, your business and with others.

It's really up to you as to whether you're prepared to do the work to help your brilliance shine more brightly and more often, to become part of your everyday, to at least appear more often than it hides.

As with anything in life, those who do the work will reap the rewards. Those who are prepared to do what the majority of people are unwilling to do experience the amplification effects of unleashing their brilliance for themselves and for others. They experience increased confidence and belief in themselves, they are able to harness the energy to maintain momentum, they surround themselves with the right people working together to drive success and they see the results in themselves, their teams, their business, their families and their lives.

As individuals, leaders, teams and businesses all wanting to do better, be better, become better, we need to be the brilliant selves we can be.

You are brilliant and your possibilities are exciting.

It's time to let your brilliance shine.

Connect with me

Thank you so much for taking the time to read this book. It has been an incredible personal journey over the past 30 years as I've battled my own inner voices and dug deep to find the courage to share my thinking and learnings.

Along the way, it's been a privilege to have been taught and guided by so many business leaders and incredible thinkers, and it's been my pleasure to share my thoughts and the words of wisdom from so many others within these pages. Trust that your perfectly imperfect brilliance is already within you and ready to shine.

If you think I could help you and/or your company unlock brilliant performance in your teams, I would love the opportunity to help them become extraordinary. I'm passionate about you leveraging the amazing talent you already have. Let's chat about running one of my programs or developing a tailored in-house program just for you.

If you want me to speak at your next conference, I'd love to help your event become one that's remembered. Please contact my speaking agent Emma McDowell at Saxton Speakers (emcdowell@saxton.com.au).

If you enjoyed reading *Be Brilliant*, you may also enjoy my other two books, *It's Who You Know* and *From Me to We*. My latest articles and regular blog are sent out in my free newsletter. Subscribers are always the first to hear about my latest books, newest programs and projects. You can sign up at janinegarner.com.au.

You may be interested to follow the stories and learnings from others by listening to my podcast *Unleashing Brilliance*, available on iTunes and SoundCloud.

I'd love you to get in touch.

The best ways to contact me are:

Email: Janine@janinegarner.com.au

Website: janinegarner.com.au

LinkedIn: janinegarner

Twitter: @janinemgarner

Instagram: janinegarner

Facebook: janinemgarner

Podcast: *Unleashing Brilliance*

Be brilliant!

References

Introduction

Knight, P 2019. *Shoe Dog*, Simon & Schuster.

Sinek, S 2011. *Start with Why: How great leaders inspire everyone to take action*, Penguin Books Ltd.

Law 1, Be You: Own your spotlight

Abele, AE & Spurk, D 2009. 'The longitudinal impact of self-efficacy and career goals on objective and subjective career success', *Journal of Vocational Behavior*, vol. 74, no. 1, pp. 53–62. Available at: www .sciencedirect.com/science/article/abs/pii/S0001879108000973.

KonMari 2019. 'The joy of sleep: an interview with Arianna Huffington'. [Blog] Thrive Global. Available at: https://thriveglobal.com/stories/benefits-sleep-interview-arianna-huffington/

Maraboli, S 2013. *Unapologetically You: Reflections on life and the human experience*, A Better Today Publishing.

Facet 1: Character

Brown, B 2010. *The Gifts of Imperfection*, Hazelden Publishing.

Garner, J 2019. 'Conversations with Paul Zahra'. [Podcast] *Unleashing Brilliance.* Available at: https://soundcloud.com/janinegarner/ep-050-conversations-with-paul

Garner, J 2019. 'Conversations with Ray Pittman President & CEO CBRE Pacific'. [Podcast] *Unleashing Brilliance.* Available at: https://soundcloud .com/janinegarner/ep-029-conversations-with-ray

Garner, J 2019. 'Conversations with Sherilyn Shackell'. [Podcast] *Unleashing Brilliance.* Available at: https://soundcloud.com/ janinegarner/ep-022-conversations-with

Handy, C 1999. *The Hungry Spirit: Beyond capitalism: A quest for purpose in the modern world*, Broadway Books.

Heifetz, R, Grashow, A & Linsky, M 2009. *The Practice of Adaptive Leadership: Tools and tactics for changing your organization and the world*, Harvard Business Review Press.

Jobs, S 2005. Commencement address delivered on 12 June, *Stanford News*. Available at: https://news.stanford.edu/2005/06/14/jobs-061505/

Kerr, J 2015. *Legacy*, Constable.

Kouchaki, M 2015. 'Fake it until you make it? Not so fast', Kellogg Insight. Available at: https://insight.kellogg.northwestern.edu/article/the-problem-with-faking-it

Obama, M 2018. *Becoming*, Viking.

Sacca, C 2011. Commencement speech, Carlson School of Management.

Facet 2: Focus

Duckworth, A 2013. *Grit: The power of passion and perseverance.* [Video recording] TED. Available at: https://www.ted.com/ talks/angela_lee_duckworth_grit_the_power_of_passion_and_perseverance?language=en

Garner, J 2019. 'Conversations with Cathy Burke | The Hunger Project | Author | Mentor'. [Podcast] *Unleashing Brilliance.* Available at: https:// soundcloud.com/janinegarner/ep-056-convesations-with-cathy

Giang, V 2013. 'This CEO is giving his employees "get out of jail free" cards', *Business Insider*.

Hill, N 1996. *Think and Grow Rich*, 5th edn, Ballantine Books.

Jobs, S 1997. Apple's 1997 Worldwide Developers Conference. Available at: https://www.cnbc.com/2018/10/02/steve-jobs-heres-what-most-people-get-wrong-about-focus.html; and https://www.forbes.com/sites/carminegallo/2011/05/16/steve-jobs-get-rid-of-the-crappy-stuff/#4ff0abad7145

Rothfuss, P 2008. *The Name of the Wind*, DAW Books.

Sapadin, L 2004. *Master Your Fears: How to triumph over your worries and get on with your life*, Wiley.

Facet 3: Expertise

Garner, J 2019. 'Conversations with Stephen Scheeler former Facebook CEO (ANZ)'. [Podcast] *Unleashing Brilliance*. Available at: https://soundcloud.com/janinegarner/ep-045-conversations-with

Gladwell, M 2008. *Outliers: The story of success*, Little, Brown and Company.

Pincus, N. *I Am Not a Genius, and So Are You,* self-published.

Law 1: Watch out!

Corkindale, G 2008. 'Overcoming imposter syndrome', *Harvard Business Review*.

Fischer, J 2016. 'LeBron James's only Achilles heel is the free-throw line', *Sports Illustrated*. Available at: https://www.si.com/nba/2016/05/17/lebron-james-cavaliers-heat-ray-allen-free-throw-line-nba-playoffs

Guerra, D & Martin, M 2017. 'Why Rick and Canyon Barry stay true to the "granny shot"', *npr*. Available at: https://www.npr.org/2017/05/28/530504774/why-rick-and-canyon-barry-stay-true-to-the-granny-shot

Patel, D 2018. '11 fears every entrepreneur must overcome', *Entrepreneur*. Available at: https://www.entrepreneur.com/article/324176

Law 2, Be Ready: Harness your energy

Facet 4: Mindset

Dweck, C 2007. *Mindset: The new psychology of success*, Ballantine Books.

Kerr, J 2015. *Legacy*, Constable.

Pride, J 2018. *Unicorn Tears: Why startups fail and how to avoid it*, Wiley.

Runyon, J 2014. 'Impossible case study: Sir Roger Bannister and the four-minute mile', *Impossible*. Available at: https://impossiblehq.com/impossible-case-study-sir-roger-bannister/

Silver, L 2019. 'Smartphone ownership is growing rapidly around the world, but not always equally', Pew Research Center. Available at: https://www.pewresearch.org/global/2019/02/05/smartphone-ownership-is-growing-rapidly-around-the-world-but-not-always-equally

Zillman, C 2019. 'The Fortune 500 has more female CEOs than ever before', *Fortune*. Available at: https://fortune.com/2019/05/16/fortune-500-female-ceos

Facet 5: Stamina

Borchard, TJ 2018. 'How to say "no" and make it stick', *PsychCentral*.

Chow, D 2013. 'Why humans are bad at multitasking', *Live Science*. Available at: https://www.livescience.com/37420-multitasking-brain-psychology.html

Evans, L 2016. 'How asking for help can be the difference between success and shutting down', *Entrepreneur*. Available at: https://www.entrepreneur.com/article/269982

Godin, S 2019. Opportunity costs just went up, [Blog] *Seth's Blog*. Available at: https://seths.blog/2019/01/opportunity-costs-just-went-up/

Huffington, A 2015. *Thrive: The third metric to redefining success and creating a life of well-being, wisdom, and wonder*, Harmony Books.

Loehr J & Schwartz, T 2007. *The Power of Full Engagement*, Free Press.

Pfeffer, J 2018. *Dying for a Paycheck: How modern management harms employee health and company performance — and what we can do about it*, HarperCollins.

RAND Corporation, 2016. 'Lack of sleep costing US economy up to $411 billion per year', *Science Daily*. Available at: https://www.sciencedaily.com/releases/2016/11/161130130826.htm

Sedaris, D 2009. 'Laugh, kookaburra', *The New Yorker*.

Williamson AM & Feyer, A 2000. 'Moderate sleep deprivation produces impairments in cognitive and motor performance equivalent to legally prescribed levels of alcohol intoxication', *Occupational and Environmental Medicine,* vol. 57, no. 10, pp. 649–55. Available at: https://www.ncbi.nlm.nih.gov/pmc/articles/PMC1739867/

Facet 6: Behaviour

AsapSCIENCE, 2018. *The science of procrastination—and how to manage it.* [Video] Available at: http://www.asapscience.com/blog/2018/5/28/how-to-stop-procrastinating-for-good

Burchard, B 2014. *The Motivation Manifesto: 9 declarations to claim your personal power,* Hay House Inc.

Clear, J 2018. *Atomic Habits: An easy and proven way to build good habits and break bad ones,* Avery.

Duhigg, C 2013. *The Power of Habit: Why we do what we do, and how to change,* Century Trade.

Fox, J 2016. *How to Lead a Quest: A handbook for pioneering executives,* Wiley.

Garner, J 2019. 'Conversations with Ray Pittman President & CEO CBRE Pacific'. [Podcast] *Unleashing Brilliance.* Available at: https://soundcloud.com/janinegarner/ep-029-conversations-with-ray

Garner, J 2019. 'Conversations with Nicole Eckels | Founder of Glasshouse Fragrances'. [Podcast] *Unleashing Brilliance.* Available at: https://soundcloud.com/janinegarner/ep-040-convesations-with

Garner, J 2019. 'Conversations with Jack Delosa, Founder The Entourage'. [Podcast] *Unleashing Brilliance*. Available at: https://soundcloud.com/janinegarner/ep-030-conversations-with-jack

Hanson, R. 'Leave the red zone', personal website. Available at: https://www.rickhanson.net/leave-the-red-zone

Institute of Managers and Leaders, 2017. Pieces of the leadership puzzle. [Blog] Available at: https://managersandleaders.com.au/blog/pieces-leadership-puzzle/

Olson, J 2016. *The Slight Edge: Turning simple disciplines into massive success & happiness*, In house Publishing.

Tracey, B 2019. '3 good habits that will change your life (expert interviews)', LinkedIn post. Available at: https://www.linkedin.com/pulse/3-good-habits-change-your-life-expert-interviews-brian-tracy

Law 2: Watch out!

Borysenko, K 2019. 'Burnout is now an officially diagnosable condition: Here's what you need to know about it', *Forbes*.

Smith, M, Segal, J & Robinson, L 2019. 'Burnout prevention and treatment', HelpGuide website. Available at: https://www.helpguide.org/articles/stress/burnout-prevention-and-recovery.htm

Thibodeaux, W 2018. 'Distractions are costing companies millions. Here's why 66 percent of workers won't talk about it', Inc.com. Available at: https://www.inc.com/wanda-thibodeaux/new-survey-shows-70-percent-of-workers-feel-distracted-heres-why.html

Wigert, B & Agrawal, S 2018. 'Employee burnout, part 1: The 5 main causes', Gallup Study. Available at: https://www.gallup.com/workplace/237059/employee-burnout-part-main-causes.aspx

Law 3, Be Together: Connect with intent

Dudley, D 2010. *Everyday Leadership*. [Video recording] TED. Available at: https://www.ted.com/talks/drew_dudley_everyday_leadership?language=en

Ferrazzi, K 2014. *Never Eat Alone: And other secrets to success, one relationship at a time*, Currency.

Facet 7: Engage

Robison, J 2019. 'Why millennials are job hopping', Gallup Study. Available at: https://www.gallup.com/workplace/267743/why-millennials-job-hopping.aspx

Garner, J 2019. 'Conversations with Ron Harvey | Retired U.S Army Veteran | Leadership Expert'. [Podcast] *Unleashing Brilliance*. Available at: https://soundcloud.com/janinegarner/ep-052-convesations-with-ron

Vaillant, GE 2015. *Triumphs of Experience: The men of the Harvard Grant Study*.

Li, J, Han, X, Wang, W, Sun, G & Cheng, Z 2018. 'How social support influences university students' academic achievement and emotional exhaustion: The mediating role of self-esteem', Learning and Individual Differences, vol. 61, pp. 120-6. Available at: https://www.sciencedirect.com/science/article/pii/S1041608017302133.

Garner, J 2019. 'Conversations with Dr Mike Perry | COO of Catalyst Executive'. [Podcast] *Unleashing Brilliance*. Available at: https://soundcloud.com/janinegarner/ep-057-conversations-with-dr

Brown, B 2018. *Dare to Lead: Brave work. Tough conversations. Whole hearts*, Vermilion.

Facet 8: Network

Grant, A 2013. *Give and Take: A revolutionary approach to success*, Phoenix.

Edelman Trust Barometer 2018. https://www.edelman.com/sites/g/files/aatuss191/files/2018-10/2018_Edelman_Trust_Barometer_Global_Report_FEB.pdf

Garner, J 2017. *It's Who You Know: How a network of 12 key people can fast-track your success*, Wiley.

Garner, J 2019. 'Conversations with Emma Isaacs Founder of Business Chicks'. [Podcast] *Unleashing Brilliance*. Available at: https://soundcloud .com/janinegarner/ep-031-conversations-with-emma

Isaacs, E 2018. *Winging It*, Macmillan Australia.

Kane, S 2015. 'From the editor: Leading like Google', *Success*.

Galindo, L 2009. *The 85% Solution: How personal accountability guarantees success—no nonsense, no excuses*, Jossey-Bass.

Facet 9: Collaborate

Coyle, D 2019. *The Culture Code: The secrets of highly successful groups*, Century.

Deloitte. 'Transitioning to the future of work and the workplace: Embracing digital culture, tools, and approaches', white paper. Available at: https://www2.deloitte.com/us/en/pages/human-capital/articles/ transitioning-to-the-future-of-work-and-the-workplace.html

Flanagan, K & Gregory, D 2019. *Forever Skills: The 12 skills to futureproof yourself, your team and your kids*, Wiley.

Garner, J 2014. *From Me to We: Why commercial collaboration is the key to future proofing business, leadership and personal success*, Wiley.

Garner, J 2019. 'Conversations with Stephen Scheeler former Facebook CEO (ANZ)'. [Podcast] *Unleashing Brilliance*. Available at: https:// soundcloud.com/janinegarner/ep-045-conversations-with

OzHarvest website. Available at: https://www.ozharvest.org

Sinek, S 2014. *Why Good Leaders Make You Feel Safe*. [Video recording] TED. Available at: https://www.ted.com/talks/simon_sinek_why_good_ leaders_make_you_feel_safe?language=en

Lockheed Martin website, 'Skunk Works origin story'. Available at: https://www.lockheedmartin.com/en-us/who-we-are/business-areas/ aeronautics/skunkworks/skunk-works-origin-story.html

Trautman, T 2014. 'Excavating the video-game industry's past', *The New Yorker*.

Velasco, R 2019. 'How Nintendo became king of the video game universe', medium.com.

Law 3: Watch out!

Worsley, AS 2018. 'Loneliness is a much more modern phenomenon than you might think' World Economic Forum. Available at: https://www.weforum.org/agenda/2018/04/a-history-of-loneliness/

Law 4, Be Heard: Magnify your influence

Garner, J 2019. 'Conversations with Melinda Cruz Founder of Miracle Babies Foundation'. [Podcast] *Unleashing Brilliance*. Available at: https://soundcloud.com/janinegarner/ep-031-conversations-with

Facet 10: Lead

Church, M 2019. *Rise Up: An evolution in leadership.* Available at: https://www.mattchurch.com/books

Garner, J 2019. 'Conversations with Michelle Gregory | Founder & Director of Promotion Products'. [Podcast] *Unleashing Brilliance*. Available at: https://soundcloud.com/janinegarner/ep-050-conversations-with

Garner, J 2019. 'Conversations with Ron Harvey | Retired U.S Army Veteran | Leadership Expert'. [Podcast] *Unleashing Brilliance*. Available at: https://soundcloud.com/janinegarner/ep-052-convesations-with-ron

Facet 11: Magnify

Christensen, CM 2010. 'How will you measure your life?' Speech to the Harvard Business School graduating class.

Elmore, T 2014. 'Is everyone a leader?' *Psychology Today*.

Fuda P & Badham, R 2011. 'Fire, snowball, mask, movie: How leaders spark and sustain change', *Harvard Business Review*.

Garner, J 2015. *From Me to We: Why commercial collaboration is the key to future proofing business, leadership and personal success*, Wiley.

Garner, J 2019. 'Conversations with Ray Pittman President & CEO CBRE Pacific'. [Podcast] *Unleashing Brilliance*. Available at: https://soundcloud .com/janinegarner/ep-029-conversations-with-ray

Garner, J 2019. 'Conversations with Weh Yeoh | Founder of OIC Cambodia'. [Podcast] *Unleashing Brilliance*. Available at: https://soundcloud.com/ janinegarner/ep-035-conversations-with-weh

Hewlett, SA 2019. 'The surprising benefits of sponsoring others at work', *Harvard Business Review*.

Officevibe, 2015. 'Employee feedback'. Available at: https://www .officevibe.com/employee-engagement-solution/employee-feedback

Murch, G 2016. *Fixing Feedback*, Wiley.

Welch, J 2009. *Winning: The ultimate business how-to book*, HarperCollins.

Wiseman, L 2014. *Rookie Smarts: Why learning beats knowing in the new game of work*, HarperBusiness.

Law 12: Accelerate

CCSU Business and Professional Development, 2017. 'The top 7 benefits of learning a new skill'. Available at: https://ccsuconed.wordpress .com/2017/01/23/the-top-7-benefits-of-learning-a-new-skill/

Godin, S 2017. Tension vs fear. [Blog] *Seth's Blog*. Available at: https:// seths.blog/2017/05/tension-vs-fear/

Marr, B 2019. 'The 10 vital skills you will need for the future of work', *Forbes*.

Netflix 2019. *Inside Bill's Brain*.

World Economic Forum 2018. 'The Future of Jobs Report 2018'. Available at: https://www.weforum.org/reports/the-future-of-jobs-report-2018

Garner, J 2019. 'Conversations with Ray Pittman President & CEO CBRE Pacific'. [Podcast] *Unleashing Brilliance*. Available at: https://soundcloud .com/janinegarner/ep-029-conversations-with-ray

Index

Also available from Janine Garner ...

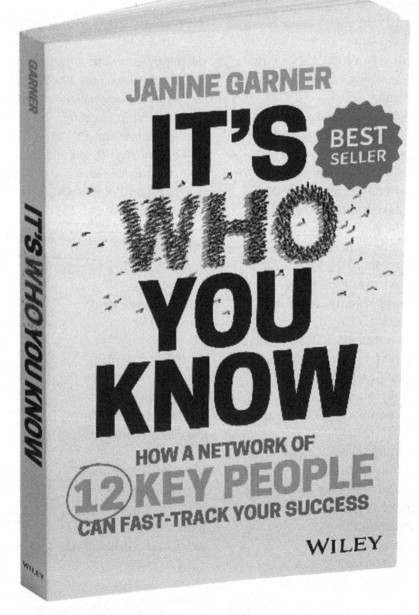

Available in print, audio and e-book formats

Also available from Janine Garner ...

Available in print, audio and e-book formats